THE BLACK BOOK

Standards of Accounting and Financial Reporting for Voluntary Health and Welfare Organizations

Fourth Edition

THE BLACK BOOK

Standards of Accounting and Financial Reporting for Voluntary Health and Welfare Organizations

Fourth Edition

NATIONAL ASSEMBLY

NATIONAL HEALTH COUNCIL

KENDALL/HUNT PUBLISHING COMPANY

4050 Westmark Drive   Dubuque, Iowa 52002

Cover images © PhotoDisc, 1998.

Library of Congress Cataloging-in-Publication Data
Standards of accounting and financial reporting for voluntary health
  and welfare organizations.—4th ed.
      p. cm.
   "National Health Council"—Cover.
   Includes index.
   At head of title: Black book.
   ISBN 0-7872-5422-3 (hard cover)
   1. Voluntary health agencies—Accounting—Standards—United
States. 2. Charities—Accounting—Standards—United States.
I. National Health Council (U.S.)   II. Title: Black book.
HF5686.C3S7   1998
657'.832—dc21   98-42652
                                      CIP

Printed in the United States of America
10 9 8 7 6 5 4 3 2 1

STANDARDS OF ACCOUNTING AND FINANCIAL REPORTING

FOR VOLUNTARY HEALTH AND WELFARE ORGANIZATIONS

Fourth Edition

STANDARDS TASK FORCE

JOHN D. CAMPBELL, CHAIR
Vice President, Finance/Chief Financial Officer
American Red Cross
Washington, D.C.

WALTER D. BRISTOL
EVP, Corporate Operations and CFO
American Heart Association
Dallas, Texas

JEAN GILBERT
National SAFE KIDS Campaign
Director of Finance and Administration
Washington, D.C.

KEVIN A. KAVANAUGH
Vice President, Financial Services
American Diabetes Association
Alexandria, Virginia

RICHARD F. LARKIN
Director
Nonprofit Industry Services Group
PricewaterhouseCoopers LLP
Falls Church, Virginia

PROJECT COORDINATOR
Nancy Reich
Director of Finance
National Health Council, Inc.
Washington, D.C.

JEFFREY D. MECHANICK
Chief Financial Officer
Planned Parenthood Federation of America
New York, New York

KATE MOORE
Chief Financial Officer
United Way of America
Alexandria, Virginia

RONALD E. MORANVILLE*
Deputy Chief Scout Executive/CFO
Boy Scouts of America
Irving, Texas

KATHRYN MORRISON
Vice President, Finance and Administration,
Chief Financial Officer
March of Dimes Birth Defects Foundation
White Plains, New York

PATRICK J. YOGUS
National Vice President for Finance
American Cancer Society, Inc.
Atlanta, Georgia

*Significant support was provided to the Task Force by Richard N. Potts, Boys Scouts of America

Contents

Foreword

The movement to establish uniform standards of accounting and financial reporting for voluntary nonprofit organizations spans over a quarter of a century. The publication of *Standards* in 1964 was a landmark event. Prior to that, these organizations had no formal guidance with respect to accounting and financial reporting. Practice varied widely at the sub-sector level of the "industry" and varied even within the sub-sectors. Since the publication of *Standards* in 1964, a measure of uniformity and consistency in reporting has developed among voluntary health and welfare organizations.

Over the years, interest in public accountability for funds used for philanthropic purposes has also increased. At the same time, *Standards* gained wide acceptance not only among affected organizations but among various funders of voluntary charities, monitoring bodies and state charity regulators.

In 1974, the American Institute of Certified Public Accountants (AICPA) published the revised industry guide called "Audits of Voluntary Health and Welfare Organizations." This guide described and effectively established the *generally accepted accounting principles* (GAAP) applicable to financial reporting by health and welfare organizations. The audit guide observed that, in most instances, these principles (GAAP) were compatible with those set forth in *Standards* and that the authors of *Standards* had advised the AICPA Committee that it was their intent to revise *Standards,* as necessary, to achieve maximum uniformity with that guide. In keeping with this commitment, *Standards* was revised in 1974 to achieve compatibility with the 1974 AICPA guide.

After the publication of the Revised 1974 *Standards,* a number of significant developments took place which led to a third edition of *Standards.* Among those developments was the creation of the Financial Accounting Standards Board (FASB) as the standard-setting body for accounting and financial reporting; the issuance in 1981 by the AICPA of *Audits of Certain Nonprofit Organizations;* and publication by the AICPA in 1987 of Statement of Position (SOP) 87-2, "Accounting for Joint Costs of Informational Materials and Activities of Not-for-Profit Organizations that Include a Fund-raising Appeal."

Thus, a project was launched to revise and publish the third edition of *Standards,* which was completed in September, 1988. These standards have supported financial reporting practices since that time, until sweeping changes were published in June, 1993, by FASB in the form of Statement of Financial Accounting Standards (SFAS) 116, Accounting for Contributions Received and Contributions Made, and SFAS 117, Financial Statements of Not-for-Profit Organizations. In addition, SFAS 124, Accounting for Certain Investments Held by Not-for-Profit Organizations was published in November, 1995. Finally, the AICPA published its new Audit and Accounting Guide, Not-for-Profit Organizations as of June 1, 1996 and SOP 98-2, "Accounting for Costs of Activities of Not-for-Profit Organizations and State and Local Governmental Entities That Include Fund Raising."

In the Fall of 1994, a *Standards* Task Force was formed, composed primarily of experts from among finance managers of major nonprofit organizations and public accountants well versed in nonprofit accounting. The Task Force met several times over the three year period and shared drafts of the manuscript with representatives of the affected organizations and standard-setting bodies. What originally began as a project to issue draft interim guidance concluded as being a complete rewrite of *Standards* due to ongoing release of new, significant pronouncements by FASB and AICPA.

The National Health Council and the National Assembly greatly appreciate the financial support for this publication provided by the American Heart Association. We would also like to thank the *Standards* Task Force for their persistence in completing *Standards* in spite of ongoing release of authoritative guidance during the period *Standards* were under revision.

With the publication of this fourth edition, we reaffirm our commitment to the highest standards of public accountability for funds used by voluntary health and welfare organizations.

MYRL WEINBERG
President
National Health
Council, Inc.

GORDON RALEY
President
National Assembly of National
Voluntary Health and Social
Welfare Organizations, Inc.

October, 1998

Standards of Accounting and Financial Reporting

The Purpose of the Revised Standards

This fourth edition of Standards of Accounting and Financial Reporting for Voluntary Health and Welfare Organizations (Standards) was prepared to continue the mission of the previous editions—to attain uniform accounting and external financial reporting in compliance with generally accepted accounting principles by all voluntary health and welfare organizations. The intended constituencies of Standards, as indicated by its title, are voluntary health and welfare organizations, including those organizations which are members of or are affiliated with the National Health Council, Inc., the National Assembly of National Voluntary Health and Social Welfare Organizations, Inc., and the United Way of America. Since 1964, Standards has guided these organizations' financial reporting. Standards has been successful in achieving uniformity and comparability of financial reporting within the industry and, with it, increased public understanding of and confidence in the organizations' financial reports. The fourth edition was necessitated by new and emerging accounting issues that have evolved over the 10 years since the third edition was published.

Standards, first published in 1964, was the original comprehensive compilation of accounting principles and financial reporting practices for voluntary health and welfare organizations. In 1967, the American Institute of Certified Public Accountants (AICPA) published the audit guide, Audits of Voluntary Health and Welfare Organizations, for the industry. This guide neither endorsed nor disagreed with Standards but stated:

The prescribed standard of accounting and reporting practices will, if consistently applied, result in reducing

Development of Standards

the variety of reporting practices since Standards provides, in general, only one method of application of certain practices.

With the publication of a revision of the AICPA audit guide in 1974, the question of varying principles appeared to be largely resolved, as indicated by the following excerpt from the audit guide:

The revised audit guide describes generally accepted accounting principles applicable to financial reporting of health and welfare organizations. In most instances, these principles are compatible with those set forth in the Standards of Accounting and Financial Reporting for Voluntary Health and Welfare Organizations. The National Health Council and the National Assembly have advised that it is their intent to revise the Standards, as necessary, to achieve the maximum possible uniformity with this guide.

As promised, the sponsors shortly thereafter revised Standards with the intent of conforming it to the 1974 revised audit guide.

After the revision of Standards in 1974, certain inconsistencies developed in practice between Standards and the 1974 audit guide. The inconsistencies developed primarily because the AICPA and the Financial Accounting Standards Board (FASB) had made significant additions to the authoritative accounting literature that affect all not-for-profit organizations. These changes prompted the 1988 revisions to Standards.

Some of the more significant issues addressed by the 1988 revisions to standards were as follows:

- New guidance was provided on the allocation of joint costs of multipurpose informational activities.

- Key provisions of FASB Concepts Statement No. 4, "Objectives of Financial Reporting by Non-business Organizations," were incorporated into Standards.

- Key provisions of FASB Concepts Statement No. 6, "Elements of Financial Statements," were incorporated into Standards.

- Applicable provisions of AICPA Statement of Position No. 78-10, "Accounting Principles and Reporting Practices for Certain Nonprofit Organizations," were incorporated into Standards.

The 1988 edition of Standards was the first to provide guidance on the authoritative status of Standards, factors in determining material departures from Standards and the applicability of Standards.

Authoritative

With regard to authoritative status, Standards does not establish "Generally Accepted Accounting Principles"—currently the function of the FASB and the AICPA—but rather, provides additional explanation of current authoritative literature and illustrations particularly applicable to voluntary health and welfare organizations. Standards focuses on general purpose financial statements; it does not include guidance for management reporting, budgeting, or data processing.

Materiality

Generally accepted accounting principles typically apply to transactions or balances which are material to the entity in question, i.e., knowledge of which would influence the judgment of an informed user of the financial statements. Similarly, the guidance and explanations in Standards are intended to apply to material items. In evaluating the materiality of departures from Standards, both quantitative and qualitative factors should be considered, such as the dollar effects, the significance of the item, the pervasiveness of the departure, and the impact of the departure taken

Authoritative Status, Materiality and Applicability

as a whole. However, because voluntary health and welfare organizations are not profit oriented, quantitative benchmarks are normally determined from bases other than excess of revenue over expenses. Other appropriate benchmarks might include revenue, expenses, or net assets by class (as applicable) or in total, or ratios such as program expenses to total expenses or fund-raising costs to contributions.

Applicability

Organizations to which Standards is applicable are essentially the same voluntary health and welfare organizations that followed the superseded AICPA audit guide, Audits of Voluntary Health and Welfare Organizations. The voluntary health and welfare audit guide defined its scope as follows (this definition is repeated in Statement of Financial Accounting Standards (SFAS) No. 117):

> "... *organizations formed for the purpose of performing voluntary services for various segments of society. They are tax-exempt (organized for the benefit of the public), supported by the public, and operated on a 'not-for-profit' basis. Most voluntary health and welfare organizations concentrate their efforts and expend their resources in an attempt to solve health and welfare problems of our society and, in many cases, those of specific individuals. As a group, voluntary health and welfare organizations include those nonprofit organizations that derive their revenue primarily from voluntary contributions from the general public to be used for general or specific purposes connected with health, welfare, or community services.*"

Difficulties in determining whether an organization meets this "definition" arise because the operative phrases, "primarily from voluntary contributions from the general public" and "health, welfare or community services," are not precisely defined (although the audit guide does say that "the general public" excludes governmental entities).

To assist in identifying those organizations that are considered to be voluntary health and welfare organizations and thus should follow Standards, the following additional guidance is given:

- Organizations that are members of or affiliated with the National Health Council, Inc., the National Assembly of National Voluntary Health and Social Welfare Organizations, Inc., and the United Way of America, should follow the provisions of Standards, unless they clearly do not meet the above definition.

- Organizations should evaluate whether a substantial amount of their revenue is normally from voluntary contributions from the general public and whether a significant part of their organization's mission includes the rendering of health, welfare or community services.

- Voluntary contributions from the general public include direct public gifts as well as allocations or transfers. The latter is a sharing of contributions from the general public with the organization from fund-raising or affiliated organizations. In most cases, amounts reported as public support on the organization's Statement of Activities would qualify as voluntary contributions. In determining whether these Standards are applicable to the organization, amounts received from private foundations, corporations or board members are normally considered voluntary contributions from the general public.

An organization should use this guidance, along with facts relevant to its own situation, when determining whether it should be classified as a voluntary health and welfare organization. Its determination should then be followed consistently unless there are significant changes in its sources of support or in the types of its program services.

It is recognized that a number of organizations that otherwise are viewed as voluntary health and welfare organizations may not receive a substantial amount of their revenues from contributions from the general public, due to receipt of significant fees from clients, governmental support or other revenue. These organizations should use these Standards to govern their financial reporting.

Need for Current Revisions

Since the revisions to Standards in 1988, the FASB has promulgated several new standards affecting not-for-profit organizations. The most prominent of these new standards are SFAS 116, "Accounting for Contributions Received and Contributions Made," SFAS 117, "Financial Statements of Not-for-Profit Organizations'," SFAS 124, "Accounting for Certain Investments Held by Not-for-Profit Organizations," and SOP 98-2, "Accounting for Cost of Activities of Not-for-Profit Organizations and State and Local Governmental Entities That Include Fund Raising." The FASB's stated purpose in promulgating these standards was to eliminate the disparity of practice in not-for-profit reporting. FASB believes that these three standards will enhance the ability of all users, both inside and outside these organizations, to understand and use the information presented.

In addition, after performing a complete review of the AICPA audit and accounting guides, "Audits of Voluntary Health and Welfare Organizations," "Accounting Principles and Reporting Practices of Certain Nonprofit Organizations," and "Audits of Certain Nonprofit Organizations," the AICPA issued in August 1996 a new, comprehensive guide, "Not-for-Profit Organizations." The objective of the AICPA project was to make the old guides consistent with SFAS 116, 117, and 124, and to provide desirable additional guidance.

Significant changes and clarifications made in this revision of Standards are as follows:

General

1. The "net assets" concept for external financial reporting is introduced.

2. Net assets must be classified into permanently restricted net assets, temporarily restricted net assets and unrestricted net assets.

3. The three net asset classes are based solely on the existence or absence of donor-imposed restrictions. These may be time or purpose restrictions.

4. The term "contribution" is defined (Chapter 3, page 26).

5. New guidance regarding contributions with donor-imposed conditions is issued.

6. The criteria for recording donated services are clarified.

7. New reporting requirements are promulgated for organizations that receive "promises to give" (also called pledges).

8. A Statement of Cash Flows is required.

Statement of Activities

1. The Statement of Activities must focus on the organization as a whole and must report the amount of the change in net assets for the period.

2. The amounts of the changes in permanently restricted net assets, temporarily restricted net assets, unrestricted net assets and total net assets are required to be reported.

3. All expenses must be reported as decreases in unrestricted net assets.

4. All revenues and expenses must be reported gross. However, investment revenues and peripheral or incidental special events may be reported net of related expenses.

5. Temporarily restricted net assets are required to be reclassified to unrestricted net assets when donor-imposed restrictions are satisfied or expire (Chapter 3, page 30).

6. Donor-restricted contributions and investment income, gains and losses whose restrictions are met in the same reporting period may be reported as unrestricted support, provided the voluntary health and welfare organization accounts for this type of activity consistently and it discloses the relevant accounting policy.

7. Payments to affiliated organizations should be functionalized if it can be determined how the funds will be applied.

Statement of Financial Position

1. A Statement of Financial Position should focus on the organization as a whole and should report the amount of its assets, liabilities and net assets.

2. Assets and liabilities should be aggregated into reasonably homogeneous groups.

3. Entities must report net asset amounts for each of three classes of net assets (permanently restricted net assets, temporarily restricted net assets and unrestricted net assets).

4. All investments are now required to be carried at fair value.

Statement of Cash Flows

The statement of cash flows is required for all not-for-profit organizations. Preparation of the statement using the direct (rather than the indirect) method is recommended for ease of understanding by financial statement readers.

Net Assets—Redefining Funds

T he use of Funds in accounting evolved from the need for orderly accounting and reporting on amounts restricted for different purposes. A Fund is a separate accounting entity with a self-balancing set of accounts for recording assets, liabilities, fund balance and changes in fund balance. The distinctive characteristics of Funds are that they are established to reflect the wishes and restrictions of contributors, or the intentions of an organization's governing board.

Statement of Financial Accounting Standards No. 117, Financial Statements of Not-for-Profit Organizations, and Statement of Financial Accounting Standards No. 116, Accounting for Contributions Received and Contributions Made, both issued June, 1993, prescribed fundamental changes in the way voluntary organizations report financial activity. Gone are the familiar "funds" that provided separate accountability for assets, liabilities, revenues, expenses and fund balances associated with transactions driven by the wishes and restrictions of the donor, as well as the type of transactions, e.g., fixed assets, used in operations.

Under the new standards, donor restrictions are still the primary factor that determines how transactions are grouped. However, for the purposes of financial reporting, funds have been replaced by classes of net assets, and the classification of transactions is largely predicated upon the application of the criteria of whether a transaction is considered a contribution or exchange, and whether the contribution or investment income is unrestricted, temporarily restricted or permanently restricted by the donor.

Ultimately, by the application of consistent, well-defined business and accounting principles across the variety of not-for-profit organizations, relevant information will be provided to meet the

Transition from Fund Accounting to Reporting by Classes of Net Assets

common interests of donors, members, creditors and others who provide resources to such organizations. For voluntary organizations, external users have two primary common interests in assessing performance, (1) the services an organization provides, and its ability to continue to provide those services, and (2) how management discharges its stewardship responsibilities. The standards enumerated in SFAS 116 and 117 continue to require disciplined accountability similar to previous authoritative literature that produced fund accounting. However, greater flexibility in presentation is allowed, as long as appropriate presentations of net asset classes are reported or disclosed.

Throughout this book, the distinction between "fund accounting" and reporting by "net asset class" should be clear. Many organizations will still *account* for financial activity with the use of funds, due to the disciplined, self-balancing nature of the accounts, and the desire to segregate financial activity related to unrestricted, donor-restricted, permanently restricted, board-designated, and other important groupings of financial activity. Consequently, when the term "funds" is used in this book, it will refer to the way an organization accounts internally for transactions. For external financial *reporting* purposes, this book will reference "net asset classes," "classes of net assets" or "net asset categories." Due to the significance of SFAS 117, it is important to make these distinctions and treat terminology consistently, even though organizations have considerable flexibility in adopting terminology that best meets their needs.

Unrestricted Net Assets

Unrestricted Net Assets

Unrestricted net assets include all unrestricted resources committed to, or currently available for use in carrying out the organization's program and supporting services. Such assets and liabilities should be distinguished from those that are temporarily or permanently restricted for use by a donor. Note that restrictions imposed solely an external authority who is not a donor (except for certain legal restrictions related to endowments) do not cause the resulting income or net assets to be reported in a restricted class of net assets. Such "restricted" amounts are reported in the unrestricted class since the restrictions were not imposed by a donor. The only exception to this rule would be those instances where governing law dictates that net investment gains be permanently restricted with the original donor corpus (see page 17).

Increases in unrestricted net assets are generally due to contributions, bequests, program service fees, dues, investment income, income from endowment funds and sales of goods and services. Decreases in unrestricted net assets generally result from expenses incurred to conduct program services (including grants and allocations) and supporting services conducted by the organization.

What follows is a general description of fund types which can be incorporated in the unrestricted net assets class:

General/Operating Fund

The general/operating fund is historically unrestricted. It includes all unrestricted resources committed to, or currently available for use, in carrying out the organization's program and supporting services. Definitions for program and supporting services are in Chapter 5.

Board-Designated Fund

Funds specifically designated by board action for a particular purpose are board-designated. Board-designated funds are included in unrestricted net assets because the board has discretionary control over the assets. The word "restricted" should not be used to describe such funds. The fund balance for board-designated funds must be included in "Total Unrestricted Net Assets" on the balance sheet. Additionally, net changes to board-designated funds must also be incorporated in "Changes in Unrestricted Net Assets" on the Statement of Activities. Examples of board-designated fund types are as follows:

Quasi-Endowments or Funds Functioning as Endowments

The corpus of a quasi-endowment is classified as an unrestricted asset because there is no donor-imposed restriction, but an organizational designation. These funds are under the control of the governing board and management. They are available for general use at the discretion of the board.

Program Fund (Unrestricted portion)

A program fund is one in which the board specifically sets aside a portion of net assets to fund a certain program, activity, or purpose, e.g., disaster relief, AIDS education, a homeless project, research, etc. Again, these funds are under the control of the governing board and management and are available for general use. Program funds resulting from donor-imposed restrictions are included in temporarily restricted net assets—below.

Unrestricted Fixed Assets Fund

In past practice, fixed assets were maintained in a separate plant fund entitled "Land, Building and Equipment Fund." Fixed assets are unrestricted when they are either purchased with unrestricted funds or contributed without restriction as to use or disposition, and the organization does not imply a time restriction on such contributions. Unrestricted fixed assets are recorded at cost less depreciation, and are offset by associated liabilities such as mortgage notes, bonds or capital leases in the unrestricted net asset class on the balance sheet.

Expended Portion of Donor-Restricted Fixed Asset (Plant) Funds

Expended donor-restricted fixed asset funds may either be unrestricted or temporarily (in rare cases permanently) restricted, depending on the accounting policies of the voluntary organization. However, the organization must be consistent in its application of plant fund designations, and must disclose its accounting policy on the treatment of expended restricted plant funds. Unexpended donor-restricted contributions for purchase of fixed assets should be recorded in the temporarily restricted net asset class.

Custodian Fund (on the balance sheet only)

Transactions related to custodian funds are not reported in the income statement, however, total custodial assets are always offset by equivalent custodial liabilities. Because such funds are not donor-restricted, the assets and liabilities should be reported *on the balance sheet only*. In a balance sheet which is fully disaggregated by class, such assets and liabilities would be reported in the unrestricted class. Cash flows related to such funds will be included with operating cash flows in the statement of cash flows. Disclosure of such funds is recommended.

Temporarily Restricted Net Assets

When a donor limits the use of a contribution, a voluntary organization has the responsibility to ensure donated assets are used in accordance with the donor's specifications. Contributions are restricted when the nature of the solicitation specifically indicates that amounts collected from the appeal will be used for a certain purpose (implied restriction). The voluntary organization must account for each distinct donor-specified purpose. The temporarily restricted net assets class is where such activities are recorded.

This net assets class represents resources currently available for use, but expendable only for purposes specified by the donor or grantor. These assets may originate from gifts, grants, income from endowment funds restricted for specific purposes by the donor (a purpose restriction) or other similar sources. Resources unrestricted as to purpose or place, but which are specified by the donor for use in a fiscal year other than the current one (a time restriction), are also recorded in the temporarily restricted net assets class.

As an organization receives increasing numbers of restricted gifts, these gifts may accumulate to the point of posing problems in maintaining a clear indication of the degree to which the donors' restrictions have been satisfied. One of the most important functions of a voluntary organization's public financial reporting is to show clearly that this is being accomplished.

When a donor-imposed time or purpose restriction is satisfied, temporarily restricted net assets are reclassified, in an amount equal to the amount expended to satisfy the organization's commitment(s) to the donor(s), as unrestricted net assets. Such amounts reclassified should never exceed the original donor-restricted contribution amounts. Accounting for reclassifications is discussed later in this chapter. What follows are general descriptions of some types of fund categories incorporated in the temporarily restricted net asset class.

Term Endowments

(This supersedes Appendix 4 in the 1988 revision of Standards) When the terms of an endowment instrument provide for eventual lifting of the restriction on the principal, then the net assets are classified as temporarily restricted until the term expires. When investment assets of a term endowment are released from restriction, such net assets are reclassified to the unrestricted net assets class.

Donor-Restricted Funds (purpose or time)

When a donor limits the use of a contribution, it must be recorded as temporarily restricted revenue and net assets until the restriction has been satisfied. Upon satisfaction of the restriction, such net assets are reclassified to the unrestricted net assets class, in the amount of the expenditure which satisfied the restriction, not to exceed the amount contributed.

Unexpended Donor-Restricted Fixed Asset (Plant) Funds

If a donor has stipulated that donated amounts are to be used for the acquisition of fixed assets, then such resources are classified as temporarily restricted net assets. Once the resources are used to acquire fixed assets, the voluntary organization should reclassify the amount expended from temporarily restricted net assets to unrestricted net assets. However, this reclassification should occur only if it is the voluntary organization's policy to consider the restriction to be released when the assets are placed in service, and if the donor did not restrict the disposition of the fixed assets after purchase.

Restricted Fixed Assets

A donor may limit the use of a contributed fixed asset or an organization may adopt a policy which implies a time restriction on donated fixed assets. Because these restrictions expire over an asset's useful life, such net assets are reported in the temporarily restricted net assets class. An organization's policy regarding the implication of a time restriction on donated fixed assets should be disclosed in the notes to the financial statements. Depreciation on temporarily restricted property and equipment is a reduction of unrestricted net assets, which causes a reclassification from temporarily restricted net assets on the statement of activities as "Net Assets Released from Restriction."

Permanently Restricted Net Assets

Permanently restricted net assets should be isolated from other net assets since they are not directly available for providing services or for payment to creditors. Revenues derived from permanently restricted assets are to be classified in the unrestricted net assets class, unless the use of such revenue is donor-restricted. In those instances, revenues should be classified as stipulated by the donor.

Permanently restricted net assets result from contributions and other inflows of assets whose use by the voluntary organization is limited by donor-imposed restrictions that neither expire by passage of time nor can be fulfilled or otherwise removed by actions of the organization. Also included in this class will be amounts used by an organization to match a donor-restricted challenge grant for permanent endowment. What follows is a general description of the fund categories incorporated in the permanently restricted net asset class.

Permanent Endowments

A permanent endowment fund accounts for the principal amount of gifts and bequests accepted with a donor stipulation that the principal be maintained intact in perpetuity, and that only the income from investment thereof be expended either for general purposes or for purposes specified by the donor.

If stipulated by the donor, investment income and gains or losses may accumulate in the endowment fund until the occurrence of a specified event, for a specified period, or until the balance reaches a specified level. If a donor specifies a particular purpose for investment income, but is silent about the status of gains or losses, the gains or losses should generally be reported in the same class as the income. Unless so stipulated, however, investment revenues are reported as income in the unrestricted net assets class. Net gains or losses from the sale of the investments or other endowed property would also be reported in the unrestricted net assets class, unless the governing board determines (after consultation with counsel) that relevant law requires the retention of net gains in the permanently restricted net assets class. The initial receipt of the principal of an endowment—the amount donated for investment—is to be reported in the appropriate public support category of the permanently restricted column of Exhibit B.

It follows that income (as opposed to capital gains) earned on endowment investments may be either unrestricted, and therefore require no differentiation from other current investment income of an entity, or be donor-restricted, in which case the income is treated as restricted revenue and reported in the temporarily (or permanently) restricted net asset class. If endowment income is not donor-restricted, it should be credited, as earned, to investment income within the unrestricted net assets class. Note that such income is *not* recorded first in permanently restricted net assets and then reclassified to temporarily restricted or unrestricted net assets.

An organization that has endowment money invested in depreciable income-producing assets has a special depreciation problem. If it is the donor's intent that the endowment's principal be maintained intact (as is generally the case), this requires that depreciation be charged as an expense against the related revenue; only the net income or loss after depreciation will be considered available for use (and thus the depreciation will not appear in the expenses section). In the balance sheet, accumulated depreciation should be treated the same way as it is for other depreciable assets, although the related assets in this case will be reported as permanently restricted net assets.

Annuity and Life-Income (Split-Interest) Funds

Annuity and life-income (or split-interest) funds are used by not-for-profit organizations to account for resources provided by donors under certain kinds of agreements in which the organization has a beneficial interest in the resources but is not the sole beneficiary. These agreements include charitable lead and remainder trusts, charitable gift annuities, and pooled (life) income funds.

Fund balances of annuity and life-income funds represent an entity's beneficial interest in the resources contributed by donors under split-interest agreements. Any portion of the fund balances representing amounts that will become part of permanent endowment when the agreements terminate should be classified as permanently restricted net assets. Any portion of the fund balances representing amounts that will be available for restricted purposes, or available for unrestricted use, by the entity only when agreements terminate should be classified as temporarily restricted net assets. Any portion of the fund balances representing amounts that are immediately available for unrestricted purposes should be classified as unrestricted net assets.

A complete discussion of these types of arrangements is in Chapter 6 of the new AICPA audit guide.

Donor-Imposed Conditions

Donor-imposed conditions differ from restrictions. A restriction is a stipulation as to the time or purpose of use of contributions already received or receivable. A condition is a circumstance prescribed by the donor that requires another uncertain event or action to occur before the organization is entitled to receive a contribution. Usually such conditional contributions are in the form of promises to give, if the stipulated event occurs.

A donor-imposed condition might include the occurrence or nonoccurrence of an event or a certain level of matching contributions. In addition, some conditions may be substantially met in stages rather than a single event. Paragraph 5.23 in the AICPA Audit and Accounting Guide, "Not-for-Profit Organizations," gives more complete guidance and examples. If it is likely the donor-imposed conditions can be met in the current accounting period, such amount should be recorded in the usual manner. If it is likely the condition will be met in a future accounting period, such amounts should not be recorded until the condition is met, at which time they will be recorded in the class of net assets appropriate to any donor-imposed *restriction* on them. If an advance payment of a conditional contribution has been received, but it is uncertain that the donor-imposed condition will be met in the current accounting period, such contributions should be recorded as deferred revenue or a refundable advance (i.e., as both an asset and an offsetting liability) until the condition is met.

If a conditional promise to give (pledge) is received, it should not be recorded. The organization must, however, disclose the nature and amount of the conditional pledge.

Standards of Accounting and Financial Reporting

The following hypothetical illustrates the accounting entries which are necessary to reclassify net assets.

Organization XXX received four contributions of $100,000 each from donors A, B, C and D. Organization XXX's mission is to fight a specific disease through research and patient services. Organization XXX's fiscal year runs from October 1 through September 30.

On June 3, 199Y, Donor A wrote a check for $100,000 with no instructions to Organization XXX. Donor B wrote a check for $100,000 with a note stating that the funds could be used after October 3, 199Y. Donor C wrote a check for $100,000 with a note stating that 80% of the funds were to be used for research grants. Donor D wrote a check for $100,000 and stated the funds were to be used toward the purchase of land for a new clinic.

The initial entry would be as follows:

Cash	$400,000	
Unrestricted Contribution		
($100,000 + (20% × $100,000))		$120,000
Temporarily Restricted Contribution		
($100,000 + $100,000 + (80% × $100,000))		$280,000

(Donor D's cash is reported separately, since it is not available for operating purposes.)

On August 5, 199Y, Organization XXX peer review committee met and awarded $85,000 in funds to researchers. The accounting entry would be as follows:

Grant Expense—Unrestricted	$85,000	
Cash (or payable)		$85,000
Temporarily Restricted net assets—Re-class	$80,000	
Unrestricted net assets—Re-class		$80,000

(to record the satisfaction of Donor C's restrictions)

On September 1, 199Y, Organization XXX purchased land for the purpose of building a new clinic. The following accounting entry was made:

| Unrestricted Asset—Land | $150,000 | |
| Cash | | $150,000 |

| Temporarily Restricted net assets—Re-class | $100,000 | |
| Unrestricted net assets—Re-class | | $100,000 |

(to record the satisfaction of Donor D's restrictions)

On October 4, 199Y, Organization XXX made the following entry:

| Temporarily Restricted net assets—Re-class | $100,000 | |
| Unrestricted net assets—Re-class | | $100,000 |

(to record the expiration of Donor B's restrictions)

The aggregate effect of such reclassifications is reported in the statement of activities, segregated by type of restriction (purpose or time).

The Operating Statements

The primary purpose of the "operating" financial statements is to provide relevant information to meet the needs of contributors, members, creditors and others. These external users of the financial statements are interested primarily in the support a voluntary health and welfare organization receives, and what it does with it—i.e., the expenses of operating the voluntary health and welfare organization's service programs and other activities. In addition, they are interested in how a voluntary health and welfare organization obtains and spends cash, its borrowings and repayment of borrowings, and other factors that may affect its liquidity. A group of statements, collectively referred to as "operating statements," is required by Statement of Financial Accounting Standards No. 117, "Financial Statements of Not-For-Profit Organizations" (SFAS No. 117), for general-purpose external financial statements of voluntary health and welfare organizations to meet these common reporting interests. These statements are:

- a Statement of Activities (Revenues, Expenses and Other Changes in Net Assets),

- a Statement of Functional Expenses (optional for all other not-for-profits but specifically required for voluntary health and welfare organizations) and

- a Statement of Cash Flows.

Note that SFAS 117 permits (but does not require) an organization to present as a subsection of its statement of activities what it defines as so-called "operating" revenues and expenses, to distinguish these items from "non-operating" or other revenues and expenses.

Examples of these statement formats for financial reporting by voluntary health and welfare organizations are presented in Chapter 8: Statement of Activities (Revenues, Expenses and Other Changes in Net Assets) (Exhibit B), Statement of Functional Expenses (Exhibit C) and Statement of Cash Flows (Exhibit D). The statements are illustrative, as explained in that chapter, and it is not expected that all voluntary health and welfare organizations will require the same number of classifications, since activities differ from organization to organization.

A brief review of these statements indicates that they differ in some respects from the formats of similar statements in general use by commercial organizations. This chapter will discuss the format of each of the exhibits and the reasons behind it.

The general purpose external financial statements discussed in this chapter are limited; they do not and cannot equally satisfy all potential users. They are useful to groups of external users, such as donors and creditors, that generally have similar needs. Regulatory bodies and others often have special purpose needs that general-purpose financial statements cannot provide. Accordingly, many voluntary health and welfare organizations also prepare special reports for purposes other than public reporting. An example is the special project report which voluntary health and welfare organizations submit to funding organizations (government agencies, foundations, etc.) to account for funds received for particular programs. These reports vary considerably in format and content, depending on the funding agency's requirements, from a simple listing of support and/or revenue and expenses to detailed printed forms, such as those often specified by government agencies. In some instances a funding organization may require a voluntary health and welfare organization to prepare a special report pursuant to specified accounting procedures that may be at variance with generally accepted accounting principles. For example, a funding organization may require that the special report be prepared on a cash basis.

Due to the variety of special report formats that organizations may be required to comply with, this book will only address general-purpose financial statement reporting in conformity with generally accepted accounting principles.

The primary purpose of a Statement of Activities is to provide relevant information about (a) the effects of transactions and other events that change the amount and nature of net assets, and (b) how the voluntary health and welfare organization's resources are used in providing various programs and supporting services of the organization as a whole.

The Statement of Activities presents the amount of change for the period in each of the three classes of net assets: permanently restricted net assets, temporarily restricted net assets and unrestricted net assets. Revenues, expenses, gains and losses increase or decrease net assets. Other transactions (e.g., reclassifications or transfers, such as expiration of donor-imposed restrictions) simultaneously increase one class of net assets and decrease another, and should be reported as separate items. Information about revenues, expenses, gains, losses and reclassifications or transfers generally is provided by aggregating items into reasonably homogeneous groups.

Revenues

All revenues are recorded as increases in unrestricted support unless use is limited by a donor's explicit stipulation, by circumstances surrounding the receipt of the contribution that make clear the donor's implicit restriction, or by law. Donor-restricted contributions are reported as restricted revenues or gains, increasing permanently restricted net assets or temporarily restricted net assets. Donor restricted contributions and investment income whose restrictions are met in the same reporting period may be reported as unrestricted support, provided the organization accounts for all such revenue consistently and it discloses the relevant accounting policy.

Exhibit B, Statement of Activities

In general, voluntary health and welfare organizations recognize three types of revenues on the Statement of Activities. They are:

- public support (contributions)

- government fees and grants and

- revenue from exchange transactions.

These revenue types are discussed below.

Public Support (contributions) Section

This section is divided into two parts; contributions received directly and contributions received indirectly. The term "contributions"—comprising contributions of various kinds, special events, bequests, amounts received from federated and nonfederated fund-raising campaigns, governments, etc.—represents charitable giving by donors to support the activities of a voluntary health and welfare organization.

A contribution is defined as an unconditional transfer of cash (or other assets) or a settlement or cancellation of its liabilities in a voluntary nonreciprocal transfer by another entity acting other than as an owner. This includes unconditional promises to give cash or other assets.

A donor-imposed condition on a transfer of assets, or a promise to give, specifies a future or uncertain event whose occurrence, or failure to occur, gives the promissory a right of return of the assets transferred or releases the promisor from its obligations to transfer assets promised. A conditional promise to give should be recognized as a contribution only when the condition(s) on which it depends is (are) substantially met (or if, as of the date the promise is first made, the possibility that the condition will not be met is remote). Conditional transfers of assets should be accounted for as liabilities (on the Balance Sheet) until the conditions have been substantially met.

Except as noted in Chapter 4 for some contributed services and some contributed collection items, contributions received are recognized as revenues or gains in the period received. Contributions received should be recognized at their fair values (see Chapter 4 for a discussion of the determination of fair value).

Contributions usually constitute the major source of revenue for voluntary health and welfare organizations. This support is essential to the continuity of the organization. The support may be received directly, or indirectly received through another entity which provides fund-raising services for participating organizations. Contributions may take the form of unrestricted gifts, restricted gifts for operating purposes, restricted gifts for the acquisition of fixed assets, or an endowment (the income from which generally provides operating revenue).

While most contributions generally are in the form of cash, or promises to give cash, other means of making a contribution are used. Thus, as further explained in Chapter 4, contributions may take the form of donated services, property, equipment and materials (including collection items) or related promises to give them. Donated property, equipment and materials should be valued and included as support. Donated services and donated collection items should only be valued and included in support if certain criteria are met (see Chapter 4).

Contributions Received Directly

This division of contributions should be used to report all support received by a voluntary health and welfare organization as a result of its own efforts—i.e., not through another organization. This includes various types of contributions, special events income and bequests.

Contributions Received Indirectly

Contributions received indirectly, as shown in Exhibit B, are segregated because of the concern of many readers that they be able to relate fund-raising efforts to funds raised. Segregation of direct and indirect contributions as shown in Exhibit B accomplishes two objectives:

1. It identifies the contributions received by a voluntary health and welfare organization which result from its own efforts or efforts of those under its direct supervision; and

2. It puts the reader on notice that fund-raising expenses incurred by the distributing organization(s) (e.g., a federated fund-raiser) and associated with indirect contributions are effectively netted against related contributions prior to distribution to the reporting entity. Consequently, in Exhibit B, the fund-raising expenses shown under supporting services primarily represent expenses incurred in obtaining contributions received directly.

Government Fees and Grants Section

The purpose of this classification is to segregate funding from government funding sources. Accordingly, revenue from all grants, contracts, and similar amounts provided to a voluntary health and welfare organization by any federal, state or local government agency to carry out programs for which the organization is responsible should be separately reported in this classification. Note that the revenue recognition principles for the various types of government funding must be appropriate to the nature of the revenue—i.e., contributions or exchange transactions, but the revenue may be reported as a single item.

Revenue from Exchange Transactions Section

Standardization of accounting and financial reporting by voluntary health and welfare organizations requires that revenue from exchange transactions be segregated between contributions and government fees and grants. The term "exchange transactions" includes amounts earned by an organization through dues, fees, sales, investments and other income-producing activities.

Since voluntary health and welfare organizations are required to provide information about gross amounts, the following guidelines should be followed when recording revenue from exchange transactions.

1. When reporting on ongoing major or central operations and activities, revenue and expenses should be recorded gross and disclosed on the face of the Statement of Activities.

2. Revenues and expenses may be reported net if they result from peripheral or incidental transactions or from other events which may be largely beyond the control of the voluntary health and welfare organization and its management. Information about their net amounts is generally adequate to understand the organization's activities. For example, an entity that sells land and buildings no longer needed for ongoing activities commonly reports that activity as a net gain or loss.

3. Investment revenues may be reported net of related expenses, such as custodial fees or advisory fees, provided the amount of expense is disclosed parenthetically on the face of the Statement of Activities or in the notes to the financial statements.

All revenue from exchange transactions should be recorded as an increase in unrestricted net assets. Gains and losses on investment and other assets (liabilities) should be reported as unrestricted revenues unless their use is temporarily or permanently restricted by explicit donor stipulation or by law. If the governing board of the voluntary health and welfare organization determines that relevant law (primarily state law) requires the organization to retain permanently some portion of gains on donor-endowed assets, that portion should be reported as an increase in permanently restricted net assets.

As noted above, expenses related to revenue from exchange transactions may be subtracted from revenue from exchange transactions and followed by a subtotal. Functional classification of those expenses may not be evident from the details provided on the face of the Statement of Activities. If this is the case, additional detail must be provided in the Statement of Functional Expenses or in the notes.

Reclassifications for Expiration of Donor-Imposed Restrictions

Expiration of donor-imposed restrictions simultaneously increases one class of net assets and decreases another. They should be reported as reclassifications of net assets separate from revenues, expenses, gains and losses, etc.

Expense Section

The expense section of the Statement of Activities includes all of a voluntary health and welfare organization's expenses (exceptions may include certain direct benefit costs and other exchange transaction expenses of the types discussed elsewhere):

The first classification of expenses represents the amounts spent by a voluntary health and welfare organization in providing the services for which it has been organized and exists—i.e., the expenses of program services. The functional expense categories for program services will vary from one organization to another, depending upon the type of services rendered. For some voluntary health and welfare organizations, a single program service category may be adequate to indicate the services provided.

The second classification contains the expenses a voluntary health and welfare organization incurs to provide the administrative and fund-raising services that support and make possible its program services—i.e., the expenses of its supporting services.

A third expense classification covers payments to affiliated organizations—e.g., those by local organizations to state/national affiliates. These payments will normally be used by the recipient affiliate for program services, management and general, and fund-raising expenses. Payments to affiliated organizations should be reported by their functional classification to the extent that it is practicable and reasonable to do so and the necessary information is available, even if it is impossible to allocate the entire amount of such payments to functions. Payments to affiliates that cannot be allocated to functions should be treated as a separate supporting service, reported on a statement of activities as a separate line item, and labeled "Unallocated payments to affiliated organizations." (See the discussion in Chapter 5.)

The format of the expense section of Exhibit B was developed to present expense information as simply and concisely as possible. Accordingly, it shows the total expenses of individual program and supporting service functions on a functional basis. All expenses are recorded as decreases in unrestricted net assets. Expiration of donor restrictions should be recorded as a reclassification of net assets from one class to another, as shown in Exhibit B. Expenses result as resources are used up, causing any restrictions related to them to expire.

Because many persons are also interested in the nature of an organization's expenses—such as salaries, rent, travel, etc.—in reporting to the public, voluntary health and welfare organizations should also provide a statement showing the composition of their functional expense totals according to the nature of the expenses. Exhibit C, Statement of Functional Expenses, has been designed for this purpose and is discussed later in this chapter. Total expenses of each function as shown on Exhibit C equals the corresponding expenses on Exhibit B.

Reporting Additional Classifications of Net Assets

A Statement of Activities may incorporate additional classifications of revenues, expenses and other changes in net assets. For example, within a class of net assets, these items may be classified as operating versus nonoperating, expendable versus nonexpendable, etc. If a measure of "operations" is used, it must be used in a set of financial statements that at a minimum shows changes in total unrestricted net assets for the period. If the use of the term "operations" is not apparent from the details on the face of the financial statement, a description of the nature of the reporting measure or items that were excluded in its determination should be disclosed in the notes to the financial statements.

Accounting Changes and Extraordinary Items

It is rare for voluntary health and welfare organizations to have accounting changes and extraordinary items. The example below shows the suggested treatment of an extraordinary item and the cumulative effect of an accounting change.

*Example of Reporting Special Situations and Other Changes
in Unrestricted Net Assets*

Excess of revenue over expense before extraordinary items and cumulative effect of a change in an accounting principle	$XXX
Extraordinary items	XXX
Cumulative effect on prior years of a change in an accounting principle	XXX
Excess of revenue over expenses before other changes in net assets	XXX

Other changes in net assets (Only used if the statement is further disaggregated as described below.)

Property and equipment acquisitions from unrestricted net assets	(XXX)
Transfer of proceeds from sales of fixed assets	XXX
Net assets, beginning of year	XXX
Net assets, end of year	$XXX

Due to the fact that accounting changes and extraordinary items occur infrequently in voluntary health and welfare organizations, Exhibit B does not illustrate those special situations.

Net Assets, Beginning of Year

Normally, these amounts will always agree with the ending net assets of the prior period. Only in unusual circumstances would beginning net assets amounts be restated. Restatement of the beginning net assets is required for a material prior-period adjustment which represents the correction of an error in prior years, and those few accounting principle changes which require restatement, typically resulting from issuance by FASB of pronouncements on matters not previously covered.

Net Assets, End of Year

These are the final amounts shown on Exhibit B. They show the amounts at the end of the year in the three net assets classes and reflect the sum of the three respective net assets balances at the beginning of the year as well as all financial activity of the year. These amounts must, of course, agree with the corresponding amounts on Exhibit A—Balance Sheet.

Expanding the Detail of Exhibit B

SFAS No. 117 establishes standards for general-purpose financial statements provided by a voluntary health and welfare organization. It requires that certain basic information be included in the financial statements: e.g., that net assets and changes in net assets are disclosed for each of three classes of net assets. Exhibit B includes all of the basic information that is required by SFAS No. 117, as well as some additional detail about the unrestricted class. The format of the Statement of Activities in Exhibit B is for illustrative purposes only. Each voluntary health and welfare organization should evaluate and decide upon a format it believes is most relevant and understandable to the various users of its external financial statements. Some areas for which alternative presentations may be appropriate include, but are not limited to:

1. Whether any classification should be subdivided into various components (e.g., subdivide the unrestricted classification into components such as current land, buildings and equipment, capital, board-designated, etc., as illustrated in Exhibit B); or,

2. What functional categories best report the results of program activities.

3. Whether explanatory material is added in parenthetic notes in Exhibit B and in other financial statements, or in notes to financial statements. Any such material should be tailored to the requirements of particular voluntary health and welfare organizations. However, they must comply with other relevant, generally accepted accounting principles.

Other Changes in Net Assets Section

This section provides for the reporting of changes affecting net assets other than public support, revenue and expenses. There are only a few types of transactions that can be properly reported here. These are discussed below:

Changes That Do Affect Total Net Assets

In the unlikely event that net assets are returned to a donor as the result of a refund of part or all of a restricted contribution, a refund made in the same period should be offset against public support. However, a refund of public support that had been recognized in a prior period should be reported as an expense or loss.

Changes That Do Not Affect Total Net Assets (Inter-fund Transfers)

Generally inter-fund transfers are not reported in a Statement of Activities because these transfers do not affect the nature of the restrictions on any of the net assets. However, if a voluntary health and welfare organization chooses to report a separate Land, Building and Equipment or Capital Fund within a net asset class, the most common change will be the transfer of resources into the Land, Building and Equipment or Capital Fund resulting from the purchase of fixed assets. If a separate fund is not reported, this type of change will not be necessary.

The need for this type of transfer results from direct purchases of fixed assets as well as principal payments on mortgages payable, capital lease obligations and other property-related debt. Because resources of a fund other than the Land, Building and Equipment or Capital Fund were used, it is necessary to transfer an amount equal to these resources to the net assets in the Land, Building and Equipment or Capital Fund from another classification of unrestricted, temporarily restricted or permanently restricted net assets.

Another type of transfer involving the Land, Building and Equipment or Capital Fund may result when fixed assets are sold. The disposal of a fixed asset may result in the receipt of cash or establishment of a receivable. The proceeds (cash and/or a receivable) should be reported as a transfer to the appropriate classification of unrestricted, temporarily restricted or permanently restricted net assets.

Exhibit C, Statement of Functional Expenses

Exhibit C is required by SFAS 117 for voluntary health and welfare organizations, and has been designed to help those reading the financial statements obtain a general understanding of the kinds of expenses included in each functional expense category shown in Exhibit B. Exhibit C reflects, for each function, the associated natural expense categories—e.g., salaries, telephone, etc.

The number of natural expense classifications has been purposely limited. Exhibit C is designed to present the major types of expenses included in each functional category while avoiding burdensome detail. The detail shown in the statement will vary from one organization to another. The statement should, however, contain sufficient detail to enable the reader to gain a general understanding of the nature of the costs of carrying out the organization's activities. The level of detail shown in Exhibit C would generally provide this understanding.

Chapter 5 includes a section that describes the particular expenses included in each of the natural expense categories illustrated in Exhibit C. For example, all costs related to building occupancy are included in occupancy, etc. Compilation of functional expense totals acceptable for reporting to the public requires that voluntary health and welfare organizations apply rational methods of functional allocation to individual expenses, or types of expense. (Appendix 1 is devoted to methods of allocation of expenses among functions.)

Exhibit D, Statement of Cash Flows

Required by SFAS 117, a statement of cash flows is a new statement for many voluntary health and welfare organizations. The primary purpose of the statement of cash flows is to provide relevant information about cash receipts and cash payments during a period. For profit business enterprises have been required to present a Statement of Cash Flows for a number of years. The guidelines for preparation of a Statement of Cash Flows are included in SFAS No. 95 "Statement of Cash Flows" (SFAS No. 95), which should be followed by voluntary health and welfare organizations.

Information provided in a Statement of Cash Flows, if used with related disclosures and information in other financial statements, should help creditors and donors to (a) assess the organization's ability to meet its obligations and its needs for external financing; (b) assess reasons for differences between changes in net assets and associated cash receipts and payments; and (c) assess the effects on a voluntary health and welfare organization's financial position of both its cash and non-cash investing and financing transactions during the period.

Cash Flows for a Voluntary Health and Welfare Organization

A Statement of Cash Flows reports the cash effects of a voluntary health and welfare organization's operations, its investing transactions and its financing transactions during a period. A reconciliation of changes in net assets to net cash flow from operating activities should be provided.

Financing Cash Flows

For voluntary health and welfare organizations, financing activities include some of the usual types of financing flows common to businesses—proceeds from borrowings and their repayment, as well as certain transactions unique to not-for-profit organizations. These latter transactions include receipts of resources that by donor stipulation must be used for long-term purposes, such as permanently restricted endowment gifts, temporarily restricted cash receipts from donors for land, building and equipment, and those not immediately available for operations, such as term endowments and gifts subject to a life interest.

Investing Cash Flows

Investing cash flows include cash transactions related to the acquisition and disposal of long-term assets such as land, buildings and equipment, and investment securities. Reporting cash receipts and disbursements resulting from the purchase and sale of securities depends on the nature of the securities and the purpose for which securities are held. Cash receipts and disbursements resulting from cash management activities such as the buying and selling of short-term cash equivalents should be reported "net," as a component of investing activities. Cash receipts and disbursements resulting from capital (e.g., long-term endowment) investing activities should be reported "gross," as components of investing activities. Further guidance on this subject is in SFAS 95.

Operating Cash Flows

All cash flows which are not financing or investing flows are reported as operating cash flows. These will normally include all cash flows relating to the day-to-day activities of the organization, revenue from unrestricted contributions and exchange transactions, and payment of operating expenses. This section of the statement can be prepared in either of two ways: direct or indirect.

The direct method presents operating cash receipts and disbursements by their principal categories, such as contributions, major types of earned income, investment income, etc., and payments to employees and suppliers. Grants paid and interest paid are also shown separately. In addition, reconciliation of change in net assets to net operating cash flows is required, although this may be presented in a footnote to the financial statements.

The indirect method shows the reconciliation of changes in net assets to operating cash flows in the body of the statement in place of the details of receipts and disbursements.

The Financial Accounting Standards Board (FASB) has concluded that "not-for-profit organizations should be encouraged to use the direct method of reporting net cash flows from operating activities and allowed to use the indirect method." (See SFAS 117, page 52, paragraph 147.)

Reporting Format

SFAS No. 95 allows voluntary health and welfare organizations to utilize either the direct or indirect method for reporting cash flows. Exhibit D includes an example of each method.

The Classification and Reporting of Public Support and Other Revenue

T his chapter deals in detail with the forms of public support and other revenue introduced in Exhibit B. The arrangement of the classifications in Exhibit B is discussed in the preceding chapter. Public support and other revenue are to be reported in the financial statements using the major classifications and appropriate categories described below. This does not mean that organizations are required to display all categories shown; rather, each organization should select those which adequately describe its support and other revenue.

Exhibit B, Statement of Activities, provides for the reporting of support and other revenue in accordance with the stipulation of donors or other outside organizations, the reason stated in the fund-raising solicitation, or if no stipulations are expressed, as unrestricted. The format also provides for the reporting, by appropriate classifications, of total support received by the organization for all purposes.

Major Classifications of Public Support

As noted in Chapter 3, the term "public support" as used in this book represents charitable giving by the public to support the activities of a voluntary health and welfare organization. It is the sum of all kinds of contributions, as defined in Chapter 3 except receipts from governments. Public support should be recorded in the accounts of the appropriate net asset class—i.e., unrestricted support in the unrestricted net asset class, restricted operating support in the temporarily restricted net asset class, and permanently restricted support, such as endowment, in the permanently restricted net asset class.

Restricted operating support can be purpose restricted or time restricted. Purpose restricted support is restricted for particular programs. Time restricted support is restricted for expenditure in future reporting periods. (A particular gift may be both purpose and time restricted if the donor so stipulates.)

Direct Support

Public support received directly by an organization should be reported in its financial statements using the following classifications or subclassifications:

Contributions (subdivided by major source, if appropriate—i.e., individuals, corporations, foundations, etc.).

Proceeds of special events.

Legacies and bequests.

Donated personal services of individual volunteers.

Donated property, equipment and material, and the use of property.

Contributions

Contributions are to include only amounts received for which the donor derives no significant direct benefits in return from the recipient organization. They are, therefore, to be distinguished from membership dues, program service fees and special events, in which payments are made in return for significant tangible benefits. Some transactions, such as payments for tickets to special fund-raising events and establishment of deferred giving arrangements, are essentially part-contribution/part-exchange transactions and should be accounted for as such.

All contributions received directly from individual donors and organizations, and not resulting from a federated fund-raising campaign or the like, are to be included in this classification. Amounts paid ostensibly for memberships, but which are, in fact, contributions, and amounts paid in excess of the rate established as a regular membership, should be accounted for as contributions.

However, "dues" payments in excess of basic dues may be reported together with true dues in a single caption if desired. (See also the "membership dues—individuals" caption).

Illustrative of sources of support to be included in the contribution category are the following:

Individuals.

Corporations and other businesses.

Foundations and trusts.

Contributors to door-to-door, mail and other solicitations conducted by an organization itself or by professional fund raisers or solicitors hired by the organization.

Fraternal, civic, social and other unrelated groups (direct contributions).

Also to be included in contributions are proceeds of special fund-raising activities other than "Special Events," which are discussed below.

As previously mentioned, the source of contributions—e.g., foundation grants—may be indicated in Exhibit B if desired. In those cases where amounts received from a specific source are significant in relation to the organization's total direct support, these amounts should be disclosed. Not to be included here, however, is support provided by governmental agencies or other support discussed in the following sections of this chapter.

Unconditional promises to give, or pledges, should be reported when received, assuming there is sufficient verifiable evidence that a promise was made and received. Such contribution revenue should be reported for the gross amount of promises to give estimated to be collectible, less a discount to reflect the present value of estimated future cash flows. Unconditional promises expected to be collected in less than one year may be

measured at their net realizable value, with the initial estimate of
uncollectibles reflected as contra-revenue. Subsequent increases
in the estimated uncollectible portion are presented as expenses
or losses. The interest element (discount portion) of the contribution should be reflected in subsequent years as contribution
revenue.

Special Events

The special events classification is provided to reflect support
and incidental revenue—e.g., paid-for advertising in printed
programs—derived from all of an organization's special fund-
raising events during the period of the report. These are events in
which something of tangible value is provided to donor participants or their designees for a payment which includes a contribution adequate to yield revenue for the sponsoring organization
over and above direct expenses. Support should also include the
net proceeds received from raffled or auctioned items that have
been donated or purchased. The value of items donated to an
auction should not be included as a direct cost since the value
received from the auction is really just a conversion of gifts in
kind into cash. On the other hand, values of items donated to a
raffle should be included as a direct benefit cost. Dinners, dances,
bazaars, card parties, fashion shows, walk-a-thons, swim-a-thons,
and candy and greeting card sales are examples of fund-raising
activities that may qualify as special events. However, such
activities may be included in the category only if the donors or
designees receive a tangible benefit in return for payments. If no
tangible benefit is received, the proceeds of the fund-raising
activity should be included in the "contributions" category or
shown in a separate caption.

Revenue from a special event should be reported gross if the
event is considered major or ongoing, but may be reported net of
direct benefit costs if the event is peripheral or incidental. Major
or ongoing events are those that are a normal part of the organization's strategy or which generate gross revenues or expenses
which are significant in relation to the organization's budget.

Standards of Accounting and Financial Reporting

Events are peripheral or incidental if they are not an integral part of the organization's usual activities or if their gross revenues or expenses are not significant in relation to the organization's annual budget. For major or ongoing events, the reporting of the direct donor benefits and other costs may be displayed as a line item deducted from the special event revenues or reported in the expense section of the Statement of Activities reflected in, or allocated to, the appropriate program or supporting function. (See Chapter 5, "Donor Benefits," for further discussion of special events expense disclosure.)

Direct benefit costs are defined as actual costs to the organization (not fair value to the recipient) of the dinner, ballroom, orchestra, decorations and refreshments in the case of a dance; of the price of admission to a theater party; of bazaar or circus prizes, etc.—i.e., the articles and services furnished as benefits directly to the donor or donor's designee. The organization should maintain records for special events that show gross proceeds separately from direct benefit costs. The fair value of the benefit to the donor is used for tax purposes to derive the deductible amount of the donor's cash payment. All other direct and indirect expenses of promoting and conducting special events are to be reported directly as fund-raising expenses. Referred to here are such expenses as printing tickets and posters, mailing, fees and expenses of public relations and fund-raising consultants, other promotional activities, and the salaries and other expenses of the sponsoring organization itself that are reasonably allocable to the planning, promotion and conducting of special events.

The reporting described above applies only to special events sponsored by the reporting organization itself, or by an organization under its control. When a completely independent organization over which the reporting organization has no control sponsors an event for the organization's benefit, the net proceeds received by the latter should be reported as contributions.

Special events support should be reported in the net asset class appropriate to any restrictions on the use of the proceeds implicit in the purpose for which the contributions were solicited, as stated in the promotional materials for the event (i.e., unrestricted, unless the event was advertised as soliciting support for a particular purpose).

Telethons

Telethons and other forms of TV and radio entertainment are not usually considered special events for public reporting purposes. Contributions received in response to such appeals are normally to be reported as public support, and expenses attributable to the appeals should be properly functionalized, assuming the telethon is a major or ongoing event.

However, under certain conditions, a telethon or similar fund-raising event could have characteristics of a special event and thus warrant "special event treatment." To qualify as a special event, the above definition states that the fund-raising activity must demonstrate that "something of tangible value is offered directly to 'donor-participants' or designees for a payment and a contribution . . . " In a hypothetical situation, an organization could receive a payment for "something of tangible value" and a contribution from someone other than the participants (similar to the payment for advertising in a printed program). The fact that a payment would be made to cover all or part of the direct costs with benefit to the payor, in other words for "something of tangible value," will justify treating these costs, to the extend paid, as direct benefit expenses.

For example, an organization arranges to conduct a telethon. It commits itself for one and one-half hours of TV time at a cost of $150,000. A commercial company offers to sponsor one-half hour of the telethon by paying $50,000. The telethon raises $200,000 in contributions from TV viewers. The telethon in this situation warrants special event treatment. The gross amount received consists of $200,000 in contributions from TV viewers and $50,000 from the sponsor, or a total of $250,000. The direct benefit cost is the $50,000 paid by the sponsor for "something of tangible value" (for exposure gained by sponsoring one-half hour of TV time). Refer to the second paragraph under Special Events above for a discussion of reporting revenue and related direct benefit costs. The remaining $100,000 of the cost of the TV time, as well as all other telethon costs, would be included in expenses as part of program services and/or supporting services.

Legacies and Bequests

This category is to be used to report all legacies and bequests. A legacy or bequest is a gift made through a will or a trust taking effect at the donor's death. The amount to be reported as legacy and bequest income should be net of legal and brokerage fees, taxes and other direct expenses incurred in clearing the organization's title to the gift or in converting the bequest to cash.

Legacies or bequests may be unrestricted or they may be restricted by the donor for specific purposes—i.e., fixed assets, geographic locations or endowment. They should be reported in the net asset class which is to be benefited. They should be reflected in the accounts of the organization only at the time that an irrevocable right to the gift has been established by the probate court and the proceeds are measurable in amount.

Since legacies and bequests are received unpredictably, they generally cannot be related to the fund-raising efforts and expenses of an organization in any given year. Nevertheless, many organizations actively seek gifts through legacies and bequests, and some spend substantial sums in doing so. Further, these gifts are often substantial in size. Both their unpredictability and their potential size make it desirable that legacies and bequests be set forth separately by all organizations to facilitate evaluation of the efforts to generate other contributions.

Many organizations receive income from trusts not under the control of the organization. A testamentary trust is a trust created by will; accordingly, the income from such a trust should be included with legacies and bequests. Income from other types of trusts might be shown as a separate item in Exhibit B, and the present value of the organization's beneficial interest in irrevocable trusts, including perpetual trusts held by third parties such as banks, should be reported as an asset on the balance sheet. Information about such trusts should be disclosed in the notes to the financial statements.

Donated Services, Donated Property, Equipment and Materials

The services of unpaid volunteers and other non-cash donations are resources sometimes more valuable to voluntary organizations than cash contributions. Free services of highly paid executives; contributions of materials ranging from used computers to tracts of land; office space furnished rent-free; publicity donated by television, radio and other media—all raise the question: should they be valued and reported in the recipient's financial statements? Uniform accounting and reporting of donated materials and services is further complicated by the diverse sources of this support. While it is usually possible for a local voluntary organization to request and receive from a national organization with which it is affiliated, realistic values for services and materials furnished free of charge by the national to the local, organizations may well encounter very real problems in attempting to measure the value of noncash donations from individuals and organizations from whom they have no right to demand any kind of accounting. This part of the chapter will consider standards of accounting and reporting for such donations from organizations and individuals.

Donated Personal Services

Voluntary organizations may benefit from independently donated services of many kinds, from fund raising by volunteers in neighborhood solicitations to the services of business executives. There are a number of accounting issues associated with donations of services by individuals or by other organizations. Would the services performed normally need to be purchased by an organization if volunteers were not available? What is a clearly measurable basis for assigning values to these services? How does the organization distinguish between services that require specialized skills and those that don't?

The difficulties just cited may explain the historical omission from many voluntary organizations' financial statements of any financial value for independently donated services. Nevertheless, it is now a requirement that donated services be included in an organization's Statement of Activities (Exhibit B) if the following criteria are met:

1. The services received create or enhance nonfinancial assets, or

2. The services received require specialized skills, are provided by individuals possessing those skills, and would typically need to be purchased if not provided by donation.

An example of services which create a nonfinancial asset would be labor by volunteers to build or renovate a building owned by the organization. Services requiring specialized skills are provided by accountants, architects, carpenters, doctors, electricians, lawyers, nurses, plumbers, teachers, and other professionals and craftspeople.

Services which do not meet the above criteria are not recorded as contributions, even though these services might constitute a significant factor in the operation of the organization. (Note that the organization's current financial *ability* to pay for the services is not to be considered in assessing whether they in fact would need to purchase them.) Examples of such services could include:

1. Supplementary efforts of volunteer workers provided directly to beneficiaries of the organization. Such activities may comprise auxiliary activities or other specific services that do not require specialized skills or would not otherwise be provided by the organization as a part of its operating program. (Examples include

"candystripers" in a hospital, parents who volunteer to tutor children in a daycare center, etc.)

2. Periodic services of volunteers or loaned executives needed for concentrated fund-raising drives.

3. Services provided by volunteers in an oversight capacity. These might, for example, include the time provided by an accountant serving on an Audit Committee for an organization whose auditors are from a separate accounting firm, or the time provided by a lawyer on the board, who in an oversight capacity, provides perspective on legal issues (but if the volunteer lawyer/board member were to be called upon to defend a lawsuit brought against the organization, then those services would meet the criteria for recording since the organization would have to hire someone to defend them).

An organization that receives contributed services should describe the programs or activities for which those services were used, including the nature and extent of contributed services received for the period and the amount recognized as revenues for the period. Organizations are encouraged to disclose the fair value of contributed services received but not recognized as revenues, if that is practical.

Donated Land, Buildings, Property, Equipment and Materials

Contributions of real estate, furnishings to be used by the organization, and other fixed assets may be categorized as follows:

- If no donor stipulations are made, the contributions may be reported as either unrestricted or temporarily restricted, depending on the organization's policy for handling such transactions. The policy should be consistently applied and disclosed in the footnotes.

- If the donor stipulates that the items contributed be used for a particular purpose or in a particular time period, the contribution should be reported as temporarily restricted.

- In certain circumstances, contributions of fixed assets may be reported as permanently restricted; for example, if a donor specifies that the proceeds of any future sale of such assets must be maintained as an endowment, or that a particular asset (such as a painting given to a museum or a piece of land given to a conservation organization) must be retained in perpetuity.

Funds contributed for the purchase of fixed assets are reported as temporarily restricted (unless permanent restrictions mentioned above apply). The general rules regarding the timing and methods of recognition and reporting of contributions, discussed in Chapter 2 also apply to donated fixed assets.

Generally, donations of land, buildings and equipment should be recorded at their fair value at date of gift. Organizations that receive the use of a building partially or completely rent-free should report, as a contribution, the difference between the rent paid and the fair rental value of the space occupied. (Although if the organization is given the use of costly and lavish space that it would not rent if it were paying for it, then the lower value of the type of facility the organization would rent is a more appropriate measure of the value to the organization of the facility actually occupied.) Objective fair rental values can usually be determined by reference to the amount charged to the previous tenant in a building or office, or in going rental values for comparable space in the same area.

Donation of the long-term use of property under a noncancelable lease amounts to a pledge of the future use of the property and should be accounted for as a contribution in the same manner as other pledges. The other side of the entry is recorded as an asset at the inception of the lease and amortized to expense each year the property is occupied.

Donated Materials

Important differences exist among voluntary health and welfare organizations in the types of donated materials that they solicit and accept, in the processing to which donated materials are subjected and in the ultimate uses of these materials. Sheltered workshops for training or employment of handicapped persons depend upon continuous solicitation and collection of discarded clothing, furniture and other household articles. Some health organizations receive costly drugs donated by pharmaceutical houses for use in their therapeutic programs. Organizations engaged in relief activities in developing countries or in disaster areas often solicit contributions of new, as well as used, equipment of various kinds. Organizations also receive gifts of items for their own use such as office equipment, vehicles, etc. Standardization of accounting is necessary not only for valuing materials received as contributions, but also for the costs of soliciting and collecting the materials and for their use, including processing and disposal costs, in an organization's activities.

Donated materials of significance which can be used or sold by the organization should be recorded at their fair market value when received. This includes inventory given to thrift shops and similar organizations. Objective measurable bases for the value may be available from sources such as proceeds from resale by the organization, price lists or market quotations (adjusted for deterioration and obsolescence), or appraisals. This recording is necessary not only to account properly for all transactions of the organization, but also to enhance stewardship control over all materials received. (Contributed collection items, such as works of art, may be an exception. See SFAS 116, paragraphs 11–13.)

If the nature of the materials is such that it is completely impossible to objectively determine a value with any degree of accuracy, they should not be recorded as contributions; used clothing received as contributions and subsequently given away, or a research collection with no commercial value might, for example, fall into this category. There is, of course, no valuation problem where donated materials are converted, essentially unchanged, into cash soon after receipt, since the cash received is an acceptable gauge of the value of the contribution.

When donated materials are used in rendering the service provided by the organization, the cost of these materials included in the service is based on the value previously recorded for the contribution. If donated materials, designated by the donor for named third-party beneficiaries, pass directly through the organization to its charitable beneficiaries, with the organization thus serving merely as an agent for the donors, the donation would not normally be recorded as a contribution, nor the distribution of the materials, as an expense.

If the amounts are significant, the value of the materials recorded as contributions and as expenses (or assets, if appropriate) should be clearly disclosed in the financial statements.

This section discusses the following categories of Exhibit B under public support received indirectly:

Collected through local member units.

Contributed by associated organizations.

Received from federated or independent, specialized fund-raising organizations.

This section discusses accounting by the ultimate recipient of such gifts. Accounting and financial reporting by entities which act as conduits or agents for donors or recipients is not discussed here because the rules applicable to such pass-through organizations have not yet been finalized by the FASB. (See "Agency Transactions" below.)

Public Support Received Indirectly

Collected through Local Member Units

Some national health and welfare organizations derive major financial support from fund-raising campaigns conducted by their unconsolidated local affiliates for support of the national and local organizations. The proceeds of such a combined national-local fund-raising campaign are commonly allocated between the local organization and its national affiliate on the basis of a predetermined ratio. In these conditions, the national organization should report its share—in effect, public support derived through efforts of the local organization expressly on its behalf—in this classification.

Contributed by Associated Organizations

This classification is to be used to report contributions from unconsolidated auxiliaries, circles, guilds and other organizations closely associated with the reporting organization, but not for membership payments in the form of dues or assessments. Further, only contributions from organizations directly related to the recipient by identity of purpose, programs or clientele should be reported here. Contributions from a sponsoring "parent" organization or from sponsoring religious bodies would also be reported here, but not contributions from unaffiliated foundations, a local civic organization or other unrelated group.

Excluded from this classification, in addition, are contributions or allocations received from federated and other fund-raising organizations, including United Ways, and such sectarian organizations as the various Catholic Charities and Jewish Federations. Contributions received by an organization from these types of fund-raising organizations belong in one of the two categories described below.

Received from Federated or Independent, Specialized Fund-Raising Organizations

All allocations, appropriations and other forms of financial support received or receivable from federated fund-raising organizations are to be reported in this classification. Federated fund-raising organizations (FFO), are defined as community and other voluntary organizations that perform all of the following primary activities:

1. Campaign for contributions, for the benefit of two or more voluntary health and/or welfare organizations, within designated geographical, religious, industrial or other communities.

2. Review requests of affiliates or other organizations seeking funding, or participation in a federated fund-raising drive, as provided for in the agreement between the FFO and its participants.

3. Distribute funds to these organizations on the basis of approved budgets or requests, community needs, or other participation agreements and arrangements.

Examples of FFOs may include United Way, United Fund, Community Chest, United Appeal, etc.

For support received from specialized fund-raising organizations that are not associated with a reporting organization as previously described (in "Contributed by Associated Organizations" and "Received from Federated Fund-raising Organizations"), another category may be used.

The timing of recording of receivables and revenue should be the same as for public support received directly. In many instances, the "receipt" from such organizations will be a "promise to give," and its receipt must be accompanied by sufficient verifiable documentation.

Revenues and Grants from Governmental Agencies

Support and other revenue that an organization receives from governmental sources may be reported in this classification. For some organizations, this may require the combining of purchase-of-services fees and contract payments from local, state and federal organizations with research and other grants from these units. The importance to private organizations of government payments of all types, and the frequent difficulty in classifying many types of payments unambiguously as either support or other revenue, make it desirable to report the total of this support and revenue in a single figure in Exhibit B, rather than to classify the payments in support or other revenue, as the case may be. Organizations may differentiate among sources and kinds of governmental support in a separate schedule keyed to this classification in Exhibit B, Statement of Activities, or subclassifications may be used in the exhibit itself. (Many governmental grants are restricted to specific programs; such amounts, if received as contributions, and not as exchange transactions, would usually be reported in the Temporarily Restricted Net Asset Class.)

Organizations which are receiving government grants as mere pass-through agents, with no discretion to determine the recipients of funds, should not report such grants as revenue. Ultimate recipients of such funds should, however, report such revenues as government grants, even though received indirectly. (See "Agency Transactions" below.)

Other Revenues

The Other Revenues Section of Exhibit B May Include:

Membership dues—individuals.

Assessments and dues—local member units.

Program service fees and net incidental revenue.

Sales of materials and services to member units.

Sales to the public.

Standards of Accounting and Financial Reporting

Investment income.

Gains (or losses) on investment transactions, or sales of other assets.

Investment Pools.

Miscellaneous revenue.

Membership Dues—Individuals

As already noted, the membership dues—individuals caption is reserved for amounts received by an organization for personal memberships that procure directly for the member tangible benefits commensurate in value with the amount of the dues. Substantial direct, private benefits may include: the use of an organization's recreational, consulting and other facilities and services; the right to participate in educational programs; the right to receive directly useful publications; or the enjoyment of a professional standing or other honor.

Voting rights alone are not sufficient to qualify a payment as a membership payment. Newsletters must, in many instances, also be rejected as an insufficient benefit to qualify a payment as a membership. If a newsletter type publication has no other function than to keep a member informed of general activities of an organization, it would not normally be considered of sufficient direct tangible benefit to classify payments received from "members" in this category.

"Contributing," "sustaining" and similar memberships implicitly require scrutiny for proper reporting. Their distinguishing titles imply there is an alternative, "regular" membership with a difference in rates charged. If the regular membership, in fact, qualifies as a true membership, as just defined, and if the benefits offered for a "contributing" or "sustaining" membership are not in fact greater, corresponding to the difference in charge, then the difference between the charge collected and the rate for a regular membership properly is accounted for as a contribution, although it may be reported together with other dues if desired.

Revenue derived from membership dues should be recognized by the organization over the period to which the dues relate. Nonrefundable initiation and life-membership fees should be recognized as revenue in the period the fees are receivable, if future dues or fees can reasonably be expected to cover the cost of future services; otherwise, the fees should be amortized to future periods, based on average membership duration, life expectancy or other appropriate methods. However, if items such as dues assessments and nonrefundable initiation fees are, in substance, contributions—and benefits are not to be provided to the member—they should be recognized as contributions in the periods in which the organization is entitled to them.

Assessments and Dues—Member Units

Amounts received by an organization from its member organizations (at the local, state and regional levels, etc.) for general membership benefits are to be reported here. Use of the classification should be restricted to revenues from dues, fair share quotas and similar assessments against member organizations to cover regular services, publications, materials and other membership benefits furnished to all member organizations of the same class. These transactions are normally exchange transactions, not contributions. As previously discussed, amounts received from fund-raising campaigns that solicit support for both the sponsoring organization and its national affiliate—the proceeds of which are divided between the two according to a predetermined formula—do not belong in the caption. Amounts received as fees for special consulting services to particular member organizations, and revenue from sales of materials ordered by and billed separately to individual organizations, should not be reported here, but should be shown under sales of materials and services to local member units.

Program Service Fees and Net Incidental Revenue

This classification includes two distinct types of revenue received from participants in an organization's programs. The first type are fees received for the organization's program services and other revenues from program-related activities. The second consists of the excess of revenues over expenses of service-related activities that are only incidental to the service. (Amounts received from governmental agencies and member organization payments for services to the organizations themselves are not to be reported here.) Either of the two types of revenue may appear alone in Exhibit B in the absence of revenue of the other type. Each will be considered separately.

Program Service Fees

This classification provides for fee payments, received either from the recipient or nongovernmental third parties, for health and welfare services furnished by an organization. Whether an organization uses schedules of fees for different services or merely requests clients to pay what they feel they can afford, as in the case of many church-related organizations, any type of payments in return for an organization's professional services belong in this classification. Some organizations account for fees by recording them at established standard rates for services rendered, then apply "allowances" to reduce the standard to the amount actually charged in each case. Such organizations should report as program service fees only the net actually charged.

Whether a particular payment should be treated as program service fees or as a contribution may raise questions for some organizations. Individuals asked to "contribute" whatever they think they can afford, in (partial) payment for an organization's services, may feel justified in reporting the payment on their income tax return as a contribution. This personal decision neither affects nor depends upon the organization's public reporting of the payment.

Program Net Incidental Revenue

The second type of revenue to be included in program service fees is revenue from activities that, although administered by it, a voluntary organization regards as secondary to its primary services. Examples are: the excess of fees collected from participants in a "pay-your-own-way outing" over bus charter and other group expenses, some organization-sponsored student conferences, provision of display space to exhibitors at conventions, and neighborhood self-improvement projects sponsored by an organization but on the periphery of its primary social service programs. Organizations generally attempt to make these activities self-supporting by charging registration fees, rental and other service charges at rates intended to cover their direct expenses and, in some instances, properly allocable administration and other indirect expenses. To the extent that such activities are considered as peripheral or incidental, their revenues and expenses are reported as net revenues (or expenses) in the Statement of Activities. However, if such activities are considered major or ongoing, their revenues and expenses should be reported at gross. (Display and disclosure guidelines are the same as for special events.)

Some of the program activities of sheltered workshops and other organizations that generate revenue will require careful review for correct classification. The expenses of revenue-producing activities that are conducted primarily as therapeutic training or for other program purposes should be grouped with an organization's program services in the expense section of Exhibit B. Since in these cases the revenue generating activity would generally be considered major and ongoing, revenue and expenses should be reported gross.

With respect to fund-raising work performed by client-workers of a sheltered workshop, wages paid to client-workers for such work should be included with other fund-raising expenses of the sheltered workshop. Contributions received from others as a result of their efforts are to be reported in full as contributions.

Sales of Materials and Services to Member Units

This classification is provided for the revenue obtained by health and welfare organizations from sales to their member organizations of publications and materials, consultation and other services. In general, it should be used by a voluntary organization to report sales and special-service fees billed to an associated health or welfare organization. Royalties and other sales-based payments to national organizations by manufacturers, related to sales of insignia and other organization-identified materials directly to local organizations for resale to bona fide individual members, are also to be reported in this classification.

Sales to the Public

Sales of program-related publications and materials to the general public are to be segregated from sales to member organizations and reported gross. Related costs and expenses—e.g., printing and mailing—should be reported in the appropriate program expense category. Sales of non-program-related items to the general public should be segregated from sales to member organizations. To the extent that such sales are considered as peripheral or incidental, their revenues and expenses are reported as net revenues (or expenses), in the Statement of Activities. However, if such activities are considered major or ongoing, their revenues and expenses should be reported at gross. (Display and disclosure guidelines are the same as for special events.)

Investment Income

A voluntary health or welfare organization may earn income from a variety of investments, from securities held for long-term or short-term investment to real estate and patents acquired through gifts or bequests and retained by the organization. In form, investment income may include interest, dividends, rent, royalties and even net earnings from activities—e.g., operation of an office building acquired through an endowment conducted solely for the production of income. All investment income of whatever type of origin (other than capital gains, as discussed in the next session) is to be summarized and reported as investment income in Exhibit B.

Income on investments of unrestricted net assets should be reported as unrestricted investment income. Income on investments of temporarily restricted net assets should also be reported as unrestricted income, unless it is specifically restricted by the donor or legally required to be used for restricted purposes.

Investment income of permanently restricted net assets such as an endowment, unless restricted to a specific purpose by terms of the gift instrument or law, is available for unrestricted purposes and should be reported as unrestricted investment income. Where the donor has restricted the use of the income from the investment of the endowment gift, such income should be reported as temporarily restricted. In no case should the investment income be reported as permanently restricted unless the donor explicitly stipulated that such income be added to the endowment principal for a specified period of time or until a specific balance is reached.

Gains (or Losses) on Investment Transactions and Sales of Other Assets

The net amount of gains or losses should be reported in gains (or losses) on investment transactions of Exhibit B, even if the net figure is a loss. If gains (losses) on sales of assets other than investment transactions are significant, the amount should be separately disclosed. Gains or losses that derive from investments of unrestricted net assets should be reported as unrestricted income on Exhibit B.

Gains or losses on investments of temporarily restricted net assets should be reported as unrestricted gains (or losses) on investments, unless they are otherwise specified by the donor, or not legally available for unrestricted purposes, in which case they should be reported as temporarily restricted.

Gains and losses from permanently restricted net assets such as endowments should be reported as increases or decreases in unrestricted net assets unless their use is temporarily or permanently restricted by explicit donor stipulations or by law. However, losses in a donor-restricted endowment fund are reported first as decreases in temporarily restricted net assets to the extent that this class contains unused temporarily restricted gains in the same fund from prior periods.

If the governing board determines that the relevant law requires the organization to retain permanently some portion of gain on investment assets of endowment funds, that amount should be reported as an increase in permanently restricted net assets. However, a legal requirement that the governing board of the organization formally vote to appropriate legally available gains does not extend any donor restriction to unappropriated gains. Such unappropriated gains are reported in the unrestricted class of net assets. Organizations should consult their attorneys as to the legal status of gains under the laws of their state.

In determining the proper accounting for endowment gains and losses, donor stipulations must take precedence. If the donor specifies that all gains and losses are available for general operations (unrestricted) or restricted for a particular program, such gains and losses should be reported as unrestricted or temporarily restricted, respectively. Likewise, if the donor specifies that gains and losses must be added to endowment principal, then such gains and losses should be reported as increases (or decreases) in permanently restricted net assets. Only when the donor is silent as to the disposition of endowment gains and losses should the board determine the requirements of relevant law.

If it is determined that the law permits expenditure of accumulated net endowment gains, the organization must identify those net gains and to the extent that such net gains are attributable to endowments that generate unrestricted income, they should be reclassified as unrestricted. If they are attributable to endowments that generate restricted income, they would also be reclassified to unrestricted either: (1) to the extent that expenses which would have met the restrictions have been previously reported as unrestricted expenses, or (2) as such expenses are incurred in the future. To the extent that expenses meeting these restrictions have not been incurred, such balances should be reclassified as temporarily restricted.

Financial statements must comply with Statement of Financial Accounting Standards No.124, Accounting for Certain Investments Held by Not-for-Profit Organizations. This statement calls for reporting investments in equity securities with a readily determinable fair value, and all debt securities at fair market value. Other types of investments continue to be valued according to the rules in the applicable old audit guide; these rules are reprinted as Appendix A to Chapter 8 of the new audit guide.

Investment Pools—Allocation of Investment Income, Capital Gains and Losses

To obtain investment flexibility, voluntary health and welfare organizations frequently pool investment of various funds in a single investment pool—e.g., a single portfolio of securities. The term "funds" as used here refers to various sources for which there is a need to maintain a record of the principal balance. These may include permanently restricted sources such as endowments, temporarily restricted sources such as term endowments, and unrestricted sources such as bequests or other items designated for investment by the board.

Because the realized and unrealized gains (losses) and income are not identified directly with the specific funds participating in the pool, it is of paramount importance that realized and unrealized gains (losses) and income be allocated equitably. To accomplish an equitable allocation, investment pools should be operated on the market-value method. Under this method, each fund is assigned a number of units based on the relationship of market value of all funds at the time the investments are pooled. Periodically, the pooled assets are valued and new unit values assigned. The new unit value is used to determine the number of units to be allocated to new funds entered in the pool or to calculate the equity of funds withdrawn from the pool. Investment pool income should be allocated to participating funds based on the number of units held by each fund.

An illustration of the operation of an investment pool can be found in Appendix 3.

Miscellaneous Revenues

This classification needs no explanation, but a word of caution may be appropriate. If the revenue of an organization has been properly classified, very little should usually remain to be shown as miscellaneous.

Public Support and/or Revenues Allocable to National Programs

See payment to affiliated organizations in Chapter 5.

Agency Transactions

Amounts received by organizations from donors who designate their gift to another, specifically named organization, may need to be classified as "agency transactions," those where the pass-through entity is acting as an agent, trustee, or intermediary on behalf of other parties. It is likely that such amounts will generally not be classified as revenue to the first recipient, but only to the named beneficiary. For further information about this issue and other issues related to agency transactions, see the discussion in FASB's proposed interpretation of FASB statement No. 116, "Transfers of Assets in Which a Not-for-Profit Organization Acts as an Agent, Trustee, or Intermediary." Note: The exposure draft dated December 29, 1995; complete final interpretation not yet issued (however FASB has issued Interpretation No. 42, covering only the circumstances where the pass-through entity possesses "variance power," that is the unilateral power to deviate from the original donor's instructions).

The Classification and Reporting of Expenses

T he operating statements described in Chapter 3 have been designed to meet the concerns of contributors and to meet several regulatory requirements:

1. To see all of an organization's expenses reported with its support and revenue in a single statement. All expenses are reported in the unrestricted class (Exhibit B).

2. To see how much it spent on each of its program functions and supporting services (Exhibit B).

3. To see the distribution of object expenses—e.g., salaries, travel, printing—among its program functions and supporting services (Exhibit C).

Contributors, contributor information and budget review groups, regulatory bodies, and trustees and officials of voluntary organizations are most interested in the cost of the various services and other activities provided by health and welfare organizations. They want to know the cost to an organization of each of its program functions and the costs of fund-raising and management and general services. To satisfy these interests, Exhibit B, the operating statement designed for public reporting by voluntary health and welfare organizations, provides for functional reporting of expenses.

The first part of this chapter describes the two major functional classifications incorporated in Exhibit B, program services and supporting services. Supporting services are further subdivided into management and general and fund-raising. It also discusses the expense classification, payments to affiliated organizations, and the reporting of exchange transactions in the financial statements. Succeeding parts of the chapter examine the problems of classifying public education, public information and fund-raising information expenses, problems of calculating and comparing fund-raising ratios, and standardization of reporting of awards and grants made by an organization. The object expense groupings of Exhibit C are discussed in the chapter's last section.

Functional reporting of expenses according to the format of Exhibit B requires that organizations combine the expenses of particular activities according to their essential purposes—i.e., program, management and general, and fund-raising. For example, an organization that recognizes operation of a summer camp as one of its distinct program functions should include in its reported camp program expenses the costs of infirmary, trading post and other auxiliary activities that are integral parts of the camping program. In some instances, it will be necessary to break down the salary of an individual among two or more program functions that the person serves—e.g., the salary of a staff physician between a camping program and the program services participated in during non-summer months. Other expenses, such as rent, materials and travel, will frequently need to be divided among the several functional purposes served. Methods of making such divisions, or allocations, are discussed in Appendix 1.

Contributed Services and Materials

Organizations have the option to record donated services and materials to the natural expense classification benefited or to create a new natural expense classification entitled "Contributed Services and Materials." Like other expenses, this category must be allocated among the several functional purposes benefited (Exhibit C). These expenses should be shown as a reduction in unrestricted net assets.

This first major expense designation in Exhibit B is a caption, or heading, under which an organization is to list its major health or welfare program service categories, the total expenses for each during the reporting period and the total of all program services.

Uniform, comparable expense reporting by voluntary organizations would be greatly advanced if it were possible to devise a satisfactory set of universal program service categories. These would have to be sufficiently definitive (as well as broad), however, to permit any organization, without distorting their significance, to fit all its program service expenses into one standard category or another. SFAS 117 and the Non-Profit Organization Audit and Accounting Guide acknowledge that the number and description of functional reporting classifications varies according to the nature of the services rendered.

Uniform Program Service Categories for Health Organizations

One group of voluntary organizations, the national voluntary health organizations that are members of the National Health Council, has recommended the use of standard program classifications for almost thirty years. The program service classifications defined by the National Health Council for its voluntary member organizations comprise five functional expense categories:

- Research

- Public health education

- Professional health education and training

- Patient services

- Community health services

These expenses are defined as follows:

The research category represents awards or grants-in-aid to support scientific studies or investigations, plus all other costs or expenses incurred while conducting a program in which new knowledge is being sought to find causes, cures and prevention for specific diseases or health problems.

The public health education category represents programs conducted for the purpose of informing the general public how to promptly recognize the symptoms of ill health, disease and/or physical disorders. Also included is the dissemination of facts and information designed to encourage periodic physical examinations and other appropriate health behaviors, reduce indifference toward health problems and eliminate unwarranted fears or misconceptions. All other costs or expenses directly related to the performance of "health" educational work also fall under this category.

The professional health education and training category represents activities or programs designed to improve the knowledge, skills and critical judgment of physicians, dentists, nurses and others engaged (directly or indirectly) in health work by keeping them abreast of new medical advancements, diagnostic techniques, etc. Also part of this category is the provision of educational opportunities for those who have displayed the interest and aptitude to enter the medical field or undertake scientific investigations, as well as expansion or improvement of health educational courses in universities or the like, and stimulation of health and/or scientific careers. In addition, all other costs or expenses incurred while endeavoring to enlarge the number and quality of medical personnel, and professional health workers in general, would be included.

The patient services category represents activities performed or programs conducted for the purpose of providing physical, emotional and other assistance to individuals afflicted with a disease or health impairment, or to their families. The category further includes the furnishing of medical care, hospitalization, equipment, drugs and other tangible items to those in need, plus all other costs or expenses incurred as a result of assisting individuals while bedridden or incapacitated.

The community services category represents activities such as the detection of disease or health problems, planning and improving community health practices, supporting clinics or other public health facilities, and conducting rehabilitative and similar programs. Also represented are all other costs or expenses incurred in performing functions, which, directly or indirectly, accrue to the community's benefit.

Organizations may wish to use categories which are slight variations from the above or are more descriptive of the organization's programs. For instance, an organization may use the title medical services instead of patient services. Or an organization may have programs better described as health and family services, disaster relief, disease prevention, detection, and treatment, among others.

The major goals are to report so that the public can understand the specific functioning of the organization and to create as much comparability as possible among health and welfare organizations.

Illustrative Program Service Definitions and Classifications

As previously indicated, functional expense reporting is a technique of accounting for expenses of activities that constitute a single service program. The usefulness of such accounting depends very much on the care with which an organization defines and relates its activities to functions. To the greatest extent possible, definitions of individual program functions should include identification of expenses of activities that benefit the particular program function. An Activity Based Management (ABM) and Activity Based Costing (ABC) approach to functional allocation is discussed further in Appendix 1.

Reporting Income Related to Program Services

Information about an organization's major programs (or segments) may be enhanced by reporting the interrelationships of program expenses and program revenues. For example, an organization might report expenses for its disabled worker program with related revenues from sales of products produced. Related nonmonetary information about program inputs, outputs and results is also helpful; for example, information about the number of disabled workers placed in private sector jobs. Generally, reporting these kinds of information is more feasible in supplementary information or management explanations, or by other methods of financial reporting. For uniform financial reporting, voluntary organizations normally report program service fees and related revenue as "program service fees and net incidental revenue," and program service expenses in an appropriate program service expense category.

Supporting Services

If diversity characterizes the program services reported by different types of voluntary organizations, all organizations can recognize certain uniform characteristics in the services that support their program services. These supporting services have traditionally been distinguished as being either management and general, or fund-raising in character. All costs incurred for supporting services must be reported as decreases in unrestricted net assets.

With the adoption of SFAS 117, reporting standards require, among other changes, that revenues and expenses from exchange transactions generally be reported on a gross basis and not netted in the financial statements. With the significant changes to the traditional financial reporting model for non-profit organizations, the Accounting Standards Executive Committee and the Not-For-Profit Organizations Committee of the AICPA (Committees) recognized that nonprofit organizations may have various kinds of functions that do not fall neatly into the program, fund-raising and management and general categories. The committees neither encouraged nor discouraged the use of other functional categories. The standards provide for the flexibility, as reporting models evolve, to include the functional reporting necessary to make financial statements relevant, understandable and meaningful. Accordingly, these guidelines include alternatives for reporting exchange transactions that are neither program, fund-raising, or management and general costs.

Management and General

All organizations, whether business concerns, governmental bureaus or charitable organizations, carry on a variety of essential activities identifiable with no one of their primary functions but indispensable to the conduct of all of them—and to an organization's corporate existence. Management and general includes an organization's expenses for these costs which are necessary to maintain an organization's corporate existence. It is an organization's expenses for these essential corporate activities that are to be totaled and shown as management and general expenses in Exhibit B.

While for internal purposes it is possible to allocate management and general costs among the fund-raising and program service expense categories under a "full absorption cost" accounting theory, the nature of corporate maintenance activities requires that for external purposes, they be reported as management and general. It is important to understand that the management and general function is to be used to reflect only the indispensable stewardship and other costs needed to maintain the entity in order to deliver services—i.e., the costs included are identified on the basis of the nature of the activities and what function they benefit, as discussed below, and not whether they are "direct" or "indirect."

The extent to which particular salaries, travel, office and other expenses can be identified as clearly management and general expenses will vary widely among organizations. In a large national organization, executive direction, financial management, overall planning and the coordination of member unit activities may individually command the full time of several executives and separate clerical staffs. In smaller organizations, single executives may devote part of their time to management functions, part to direct program activities and part to fund-raising. The salary of these persons will need to be charged, along with that of a secretary and other time-related expenses, such as travel, to each activity on the basis of the time devoted to each.

The advent of the information age and the accompanying technologies has led to many nonprofit organizations reengineering the ways in which the nonprofit organization carries out its mission. Program services that were traditionally staff intensive (educating the public, for example) may now be accomplished through investment in technology and the infrastructure to support it. Many program costs are now integral in infrastructure that at one time was associated largely with management and general costs. Consequently, nonprofit organizations are faced with developing better systems to more accurately determine the full costs of delivering services and products. As the reporting requirements and information needs grow more complex, nonprofit organizations are faced with implementing systems that will respond to those needs while at the same time reducing the onerous accounting burdens and complexities. Appendix 1 provides insights into utilizing Activity Based Costing/Activity Based Management techniques to address these issues.

Regardless of size or structure, the function of management and general services exists in every organization.

The following list is representative of common activities that may contain elements of program activities as well as management and general activities.

- General board and committee meetings

- Executive direction and corporate planning

- General staff meetings

- Office management

- Corporate legal services

- Personnel procurement

- Purchasing and distribution of materials

- Receptionist, switchboard, mail distribution, filing and other office services

- Organization and procedure studies

- Accounting, auditing, budgeting and external financial reporting

- Information technology

- Internal financial and management reporting.

The following guidelines are intended to allow for more accurate and consistent reporting of management and general costs by member organizations.

BASIC DEFINITIONS

Core Management and General Activities—Costs that have no cause and effect or direct relationship to any program of the organization. Costs which are inherent to the oversight and overall administration of the organization.

Traceable Management and Administration Activities— Any cost that is directly traceable to a specific program within the nonprofit's organization's mission, and would not have been incurred had it not been for the organization's involvement in that program, and which can ultimately be measured and allocated or directly charged to that program.

Guidelines for Reporting Management and General Costs

The following guidelines are provided for common activities that include elements of core management and general activities, as well as management and administrative activities that are directly traceable to program services and would not have been incurred except for the organization's involvement in the program.

Activity: General board and committee meetings—policy making and oversight function

Core Management and General—Volunteer board and committee meetings focusing on organizational-wide policy making and oversight function.

Traceable Management and Administrative Costs—Volunteer committee meetings specifically involved in a program activity, such as providing services to clients.

Allocation Methods—All costs associated with conducting and attending volunteer committee meetings that are directly related to those program activities should be charged to those activities. Costs would include all staff costs and attendee travel expenses, and other reimbursement of out-of-pocket expenses incurred in the conduct of the meeting.

Activity: Executive direction and corporate planning

Core Management and General—Organization's executive and executive support staff salaries, benefits, space costs, etc., related to the executive oversight activity. Organizational planning and resource allocation and budgeting.

Traceable Management and Administrative Costs—Administrative time spent directly supervising or working on a program or fund-raising activity. Planning and budgeting activities related to a specific program.

Allocation Methods—Time sheet or other operational measures to allocate executive and supporting staff time and related expenses to program where there is direct supervision or participation. Activity-based costing with the entire activity allocated pursuant to operational measures relating to the programs benefited.

Activity: General staff meetings

Typically a meeting in which staff representing all program and supporting service activities are present. The meeting is necessary for the effective conduct of all of the activities of the organization program as well as supporting services. Staff from the various program and supporting areas are present to enhance their ability to effectively function in their particular activities. Accordingly, the time spent by staff at this meeting should be charged to a program or supporting service area based upon the staff person's major function(s).

Core Management and General—The core management and general components of this meeting would be the costs of staff who typically have little or no traceable program or fund-raising function. An example may be a general accountant with no activities that are specifically necessary to a given program.

Traceable Management and Administrative Costs—The cost of the staff whose activities benefit both program areas and supporting services (i.e., are clearly traceable and are unique and necessary components to the programs benefited) should be allocated to all of the activities benefited (e.g., an accounting application that exists solely to support a patient service program or research grant program). Non staff costs of a meeting that cannot be identified with a particular staff should reflect the allocation relating to staff costs.

Allocation Methods—The cost of staff whose efforts benefit multiple programs should be allocated based upon an allocation model that reflects their job descriptions, or on a model that is based upon measurable operating data that bears a direct relationship to the activities benefited. For example, the salary of a computer programmer could be allocated based upon the nature of the programs being written or maintained. Depending upon the complexity and number of activities, time reporting may be necessary to provide a verifiable basis for allocation.

Activity: Office management

Represents all of the administrative activities that are necessary for the effective conduct of all of the activities of the organization program as well as supporting services.

Core Management and General—The core management and general components of office management would be the costs of staff who typically have little or no traceable program or fund-raising functions. An example may be a general accountant with no activities that are specifically necessary to the conduct of a given program activity.

Traceable Management and Administrative Costs—The cost of staff whose activities benefit both program areas and supporting services (i.e., are clearly traceable to the activities benefited) should be directly charged or allocated to all of the activities benefited. For example, the costs of a meetings and travel coordinator should be charged to the program or supporting activity matching the purpose of the meeting. Arranging a board meeting is management and general while arranging a meeting of research proposal reviewers is charged to the research activity.

Allocation Methods—The costs of staff whose efforts benefit multiple programs should be allocated based upon an allocation model that reflects their job descriptions or on a model that is based upon measurable operating data that bears a direct relationship to the activities benefited. For example, the salary of a computer programmer could be allocated based upon the nature of the programs being written or maintained. The salary of a meetings and travel coordinator should be charged based upon the activity being benefited by the meeting being coordinated. Depending upon the complexity and number of activities, time reporting may be necessary to provide a verifiable basis for allocation.

Activity: Corporate legal services

Core Management and General—All external and in-house legal costs not directly traceable to specific programs or fund-raising activities.

Traceable Management and Administrative Costs—All external and in-house legal costs associated with specific programs, for example, the legal costs associated with determining the potential liabilities associated with running a camp for disabled children.

Allocation Methods—External legal costs incurred for the benefit of specific programs such as specific charges itemized on attorney's bill. In-house legal costs incurred for the benefit of specific programs such as direct costs incurred by the legal department. Allocation of indirect costs based upon time spent on program-related matter(s).

Activity: Human resources/personnel procurement

Core Management and General—All costs except for any costs directly traceable to specific programs or fund-raising activities.

Traceable Management and Administrative Costs—Costs that are incurred only as a result of a specific program (e.g., fund-raising training, personnel search for a research position, etc.).

Allocation Methods—Actual expenditures that are identifiable with a specific program.

Activity: Purchasing and distribution of materials

Core Management and General—Any materials not program-specific and costs associated with distributing those materials.

Traceable Management and Administrative Costs—All program-specific materials, and related costs to distribute those materials, where efforts of the purchasing program are necessary in order to support the program.

Allocation Methods—Identification of specific program materials. Track costs to distribute based on measurable operational data (e.g., actual mailings, allocation of procurement and distribution personnel time, based upon time spent on program-related purchases/mailing, etc.).

> *Activity: Receptionist, switchboard, mail distribution, filing and other office services. Represents specific administrative activities that are necessary for the effective conduct of all of the activities of the organization . . . program as well as supporting services.*

Core Management and General—The core management and general components of these categories of services includes the costs of staff who typically have little or no traceable program or fund-raising function. An example may be a receptionist with no activities that are specifically traceable and necessary to the conduct of a given program activity.

Traceable Management and Administrative Costs—The cost of staff whose activities benefit both program areas and supporting services (i.e., are clearly traceable and necessary to the activities benefited) should be directly charged or allocated based on operational data to all of the activities benefited.

> The governing principle in determining whether costs of this nature should be charged to a program function is whether a cause and effect relationship can be established between the program activity and the service.

> The costs for a mailroom that collated, bound and distributed huge numbers of voluminous research proposals is a legitimate and necessary cost of the research program, and such costs should be appropriately charged to research.

A receptionist who was assigned the duty of answering patient service calls under the training and supervision of patient service professionals is a legitimate and necessary cost of the patient service program, and such costs should be appropriately charged to patient services program.

Allocation Methods—The cost of the staff whose efforts benefit multiple programs should be allocated based upon an allocation model that reflects their job descriptions or on a model that is based upon operating data that bears a direct relationship to the activities benefited. Depending upon the complexity and number of activities, time reporting may be necessary to provide a verifiable basis for allocation.

Activity: Organization and procedural studies

Core Management and General—Costs attributable to an organization-wide study (i.e., restructuring). Any procedural studies that are not related to enhancement of a specific program.

Traceable Management and Administrative Costs— Procedural study costs that are related to a specific program to make a program more efficient and effective.

Allocation Methods—Actual costs related to the specific studies.

Activity: Accounting, auditing, budgeting and external reporting

Core Management and General—External auditing and reporting fees associated with an organization-wide audit. All organizational budgeting and internal audit costs. Accounting department costs not attributable to specific program or fundraising.

Traceable Management and Administrative Costs— External audit fees that are mandated (i.e., the cost would not exist except for the program audit requirement) by a government organization are traceable to a government grant or program specific activities (e.g., A-133 Single Audit, programmatic audit, etc.).

Accounting department costs that are an integral component of the organization's involvement in a specific program (e.g., grant administration or fund-raising) which would not exist except for the program audit requirement.

Allocation Methods—Actual A-133 audit fee. Actual costs directly attributable to programs or fund-raising (e.g., salaries, postage, printing, etc.).

Activity: Information technology

Core Management and General—All costs associated with information systems (equipment, personnel and software costs) that cannot be traceable to a specific program.

Traceable Management and Administrative Costs—Costs associated with the information systems department from computer equipment, software and personnel costs directly attributable to program specific activities.

Allocation Methods—Allocate personnel costs based on time studies or other operational data to determine costs incurred as the result of program-related activities. Allocate software costs and hardware costs based on hardware utilization (i.e., the computer is used to support program activities 90% of the time). Depending upon the complexity and number of activities, time reporting may be necessary to provide a verifiable basis for allocation.

Activity: Internal financial and management reporting

Core Management and General—Cost associated with internal financial and management reporting, even though part of the finance staff time, would be spent in directly recording activity associated with programs.

Traceable Management and Administrative Costs—Finance costs associated with preparation for an A-133 audit or federal or state program audits. Costs associated with finance employees whose time is specifically identifiable with a program or fund-raising activity and exits to support the specific needs of the program.

Allocation Methods—Time sheets or other operational measures to value the costs associated with preparing for the A-133 or program audit. Direct and associated costs related to program or fund-raising accountants.

The costs of activities other than those listed above should be charged to the appropriate fund-raising or program service categories.

Internal financial and management, or administrative reporting—the last of the above-listed management and general activities—requires explanation and definition. Because of its close relation to public information, public relations and other types of public reporting by voluntary agencies, discussion of administrative reporting has been deferred to the section that deals with classification of all of an organization's informational activities.

Fund-Raising

Fund-raising activity is vital and indispensable for almost every voluntary organization. In type and scope, fund-raising efforts of individual voluntary organizations range from nationwide appeals, employing virtually all of the persuasive techniques of major product advertising campaigns, to one or two appearances before budget committees of federated fund-raising organizations that have assumed the fund-raising responsibility for an organization.

Voluntary health and welfare organizations are expected to report as fund-raising the expenses of all activities that constitute an appeal for financial support. By their own nature, fund-raising efforts may include a very wide range of activities. Illustrative of some types of fund-raising activities are:

1. Publicizing fund-raising campaigns and special events—e.g., by paid public relations counselors; by printed, radio and TV material; in meetings with potential contributors; through campaign "kick-off" dinners.

2. Conducting fund-raising campaigns, including services of fund-raising consultants; purchasing, preparing and maintaining mailing lists; recruiting and training volunteer solicitors and other campaign workers; solicitations in person or by mail; acquisition and distribution of seals and other enclosures with appeals for funds, of campaign kits, of coin containers and of other fund-raising materials.

3. Participation in local federated and federal service fund-raising campaigns including attendance at pre-campaign budget reviews.

4. Participation by employees of the organization bene-fited in fund-raising special events.

5. Solicitation of bequests, foundation grants and other special gifts—e.g., from corporations, from affluent individuals.

6. Clinics, workshops and other activities for improving fund-raising techniques.

7. Preparation and distribution of fund-raising manuals and instructions.

Object costs of the activities would include expenses of transmitting appeals to the public, such as postage and salaries (or portions of salaries) of personnel connected with the campaign who are engaged in addressing envelopes and maintenance of mailing lists.

Criteria for differentiating among and reporting activities that combine fund-raising, educational and other kinds of information are examined in the second part of this chapter. Fund-raising services and materials purchased from affiliates should be charged to the fund raising function.

Federated fund-raising organizations (as described in Appendix 2) have a unique reporting problem because of their very nature. Therefore, they should use the reporting technique described in Appendix 2.

Fund-raising efforts of one year, such as those made to obtain bequests or to compile a mailing list of prospective contributors, often result in contributions in future years. While the underlying accounting concept of matching revenues and expenses in the same period would theoretically justify deferral of fund-raising expenses in these circumstances, the uncertainty regarding the amount, if any, of such future contributions normally precludes deferral. Accordingly, fund-raising expenses should be expended as incurred.

As has been discussed, the nature of program activities varies widely among voluntary health and welfare organizations, including those which utilize standard program categories. Accordingly, it is recommended that a brief description of each program and supporting service functional expense category be included in the statement of activities or the notes to the financial statements. This will help to clarify the designations between program and supporting service expenses as well as provide the reader with a more complete understanding of the program service categories.

Disclosure of Nature of Functional Expenses

Exchange Transactions

Exchange transactions are reciprocal transfers in which each party receives and sacrifices something of equal value; as opposed to a nonreciprocal charitable transaction in which a donor provides resources to support the nonprofit organization's mission and expects to receive nothing of direct value in exchange. Costs related to exchange transactions that benefit the nonprofit organization or the beneficiaries of the nonprofit organization's programs, should be included with the nonprofit organization's program or supporting service expenses.

Costs of exchange transactions which benefit only the recipient of the exchange on a value for value basis and not the nonprofit organization's programs or service beneficiaries, should be reported separately as an exchange transaction or otherwise described to clearly disclose the value for the value nature of the transaction.

The related revenues from exchange transactions are earned revenues and should not be included in the total of Public Support on the Statement of Activities. The standards provide flexibility in displaying the results of exchange transactions in the statement of activities as long as the gross expenses and gross revenues are disclosed. The transactions may be reported net if they are nonrecurring and incidental to the ongoing operations of the nonprofit organization.

Donor Benefits

FASB Statement No. 117 requires that donor benefits *costs* be shown on the statement of activities displayed either (1) as a line item deducted from special event proceeds, or (2) in the same section of the statement of activities as are other programs or supporting services, and allocated, if necessary, among those various functions, or (3) report the exchange revenue (representing the fair value the participant paid for the benefits received) and the contribution (representing the excess of the payment over the fair value) separately; and report the direct benefit expense separately.

Conversion of Nonmonetary Contributions to Cash

Prior to adoption of SFAS 116 and 117, the charitable contribution of a nonmonetary asset (i.e., an automobile) was typically recorded at its net realizable value; i.e., its fair market value less expenses to sell. A car worth $1,000 with selling expenses of $200 would have been recorded as public support of $800. Under the new standards, the charitable gift of the car for fair value (i.e., the exchange transaction) is recorded as sales revenue of $1,000, cost of sales of $1,000 and selling expenses of $200. The conversion of a gift of nonmonetary assets to cash may be recorded net under the new standards only if it is a nonrecurring and incidental activity. Costs associated with the solicitation of the charitable gift (the car) are fund-raising costs. Costs associated with selling the car in a value for value exchange are not fund-raising costs and may be reported as cost of sales, exchange transaction expenses or some other designation that clearly differentiates the exchange transaction from the charitable transaction. The effect on fund balance is the same under the new rules as under the old model.

Fair Value Exchanges of Goods and Services Benefiting Recipient Only

Prior to adoption of SFAS 116 and 117, revenues and expenses from exchange transactions that were essentially unrelated to the nonprofit organization's program or supporting services were typically recorded net in the statement of activity. For example, if a nonprofit organization rented part of its building to a third party, the related revenues were reported as a reduction in the occupancy expense since the nonprofit organization did not occupy the space. Under new standards which require gross reporting of revenues and expenses, the rental revenues are reported as earned revenues and the related expenses are reported as exchange expenses or otherwise clearly disclosed. Reporting the expenses as the nonprofit organization's occupancy expense would overstate that expense category if the amounts were material.

Fair Value Exchanges of Goods and Services Benefiting the Nonprofit Organization or the Nonprofit Organization's Service Beneficiaries

The revenues from sales of goods or services which are related to the nonprofit organization's program or supporting services should be recorded gross as earned revenues. The associated expenses, for example, the cost of program materials, should be charged to the program area benefited.

Payments to Affiliated Organizations

This expense classification is used to report certain types of payments to organizations "affiliated with"—closely related to—a reporting organization. Payments to an affiliate include either payments from the national organization to its affiliates or vice versa. (See Exhibit B.) Payments to affiliated organizations should be reported by their functional classification to the extent that it is practical and reasonable to do so and the necessary information is available, even if it is impossible to allocate the entire amount of such payments to functions. Payments to affiliates that cannot be allocated to functions should be treated as a separate supporting service, reported on a statement of activities as a separate line item, and labeled "unallocated payments to affiliated organizations." If a reasonable allocation methodology can be developed, such amounts can be reported by function or a footnote disclosure of the purposes for which such amounts are used can be made, if desired. Purchases of goods and services are to be treated as expenses in the usual manner. Membership dues are explained in detail later in the chapter.

The discussion on awards and grants, later in this chapter, explains that an organization's expenses in support of specific programs may, under certain special conditions, be included in an appropriate program service classification, even though made to an affiliated organization. Payments to an affiliate for fund-raising expenses that the latter has incurred on behalf of the organization are to be reported as fund-raising.

Among the most difficult of expense reporting problems confronting voluntary health and welfare organizations are those of accounting for materials and activities that may be described as "public education," "public information," "public relations," "publicity" and "fund-raising." The gradation of meaning and connotations between these terms and the activities that they encompass suggests the complexity of the definition and expense reporting problem. Standards for distinguishing among these activities (and materials), and for uniform accounting and reporting of expenses that inextricably involve two or more of them, are critical to fair financial reporting.

Criteria for Classifying Information Programs

As was earlier stated, functional reporting of an organization's expenses requires that they be grouped according to the activities for which they were incurred, and that expenses of particular activities be combined according to the program or purpose served. For example, the cost of a leaflet devoted exclusively to the nature and treatment of a disease, and distributed to the public primarily in doctors' offices or in hospitals, should be reported as public education. On the other hand, a folder on an organization's summer recreational activities for underprivileged children might be fully justifiable as expenses of the recreational program if distributed primarily among schools; distributed primarily to an audience of highly paid executives, however, it would normally have to be recognized as fund-raising.

All circumstances surrounding certain activities and use of certain materials will need to be examined to determine their real purpose. Particular information pieces may be apparently educational in content, and yet be intended and used for no other purpose than to create an attitude of sympathy and receptivity toward a subsequent appeal for financial support— their real reason for distribution. On occasion, materials will have a real joint purpose and expenses should be allocated accordingly.

Differentiating among Fund-Raising, Public Education and Other Information Materials and Activities

Public Education

For the purpose of uniform public reporting, public education is to be precisely defined and reported as a separate program function, as explained below.

Public education consists of information materials and activities:

1. Describing the symptoms of ill health, disease and physical or social disorders, or

2. Describing progress made in preventing or alleviating health or welfare problems, or

3. Describing actions to be taken by individuals or groups to prevent or alleviate personal or community health and welfare problems

and

Directed either to the general public or to special groups that may have a special need or special interest in the problem.

Public education is thus to be restricted to materials and activities that are problem—and not organization—oriented, and to efforts to tell individuals what they can or should do about a problem, not what an organization does or can do through available services.

Typical of materials and activities that should normally be accounted for as public education are the following:

- School health lectures, posters, kits, etc.

- Newspaper and magazine articles on health and welfare problems

- Teacher-training programs and materials

- Health problem checklists, leaflets, models, etc.

- Health or welfare handbooks and manuals for public distribution

- Surveys for evaluation of education campaigns

Program Information for Participants and Leaders

Among the most important organization-oriented information programs of many organizations are those designed to interest particular groups in participating in or conducting one or another of an organization's primary service programs, such as day nurseries for children, recreation for senior citizens, etc. Such participating membership and leadership procurement activities or campaigns are often necessary program activities. They are to be accounted for, however, not as public education, but rather as expenses of the particular service or services to which they relate.

Fund-Raising Information

It is evident that even the most obviously educational publications, news releases and other informational activities of voluntary organizations may also have fund-raising value, if only as demonstrations of an organization's real service to the public and therefore entitlement to public support. The fund-raising expense category can become very misleading, however, unless the information materials and activities which are included are restricted to those that are explicitly fund-raising.

Administrative Reporting

Almost every voluntary health and welfare organization engages in some reporting and information programs that relate to the organization's services but that are not education, program-supporting nor fund-raising in terms of the above definitions. Representative of such reporting are printed annual reports, certain types of newsletters, and announcements of board and committee appointments and of research grants. The value of these reports and announcements in keeping an organization's name before the public, in drawing attention to its achievements and, therefore, in promoting public interest in, and subsequent financial support of, an organization is indisputable. It is equally clear that they also represent ways in which organizations discharge their proper and necessary obligation to account to the public for their stewardship of contributors' support.

Such general reporting may be referred to as "administrative reporting"—information materials and activities that:

1. Provide stewardship reporting on an organization in terms of service program and related achievements, and of professional, volunteer and financial resources used, or that

2. Provide general information directly related to their responsibilities to professional staff members, to volunteers working in and supervising an organization's service programs, and to others.

Illustrative of the first type are annual reports and meetings, newsletters and other bulletins that serve to keep an organization's constituency (including key community leaders and contributors) informed of its activities. House organs, bulletins and other pieces addressed primarily to professional staff members and to volunteers participating in an organization's service program are examples of the second type.

The broad distribution of many forms of administrative reporting and their emphasis upon the activities of the sponsoring organization, as well as upon the health or welfare problems that are its concern, inevitably give them strong public relations and publicity value. Inescapably, administrative reporting also serves public information, institutional advertising and, therefore, fund-raising ends.

There is a real problem in classifying public information materials and activities that are neither explicitly and purely education—as previously defined—nor directly or specifically fund raising in character. It is no more practical to account separately for the fund-raising and administrative reporting components of a single annual report than it is, say, to segregate the costs of the packaging and advertising elements of an oatmeal box.

How, then, should the costs of information materials and activities that combine elements of public education, administrative reporting and potential future fund-raising be accounted for in an organization's published financial statements? The logical basis for accounting for and reporting such activities is that they are general in purpose, supporting several of an organization's primary services (including fund-raising)—and comparable, therefore, with the management and general expenses. Thus, administrative reporting and other noneducational, nonprogram and nonfund-raising (as previously defined, in each instance) information materials and activities are to be accounted for in an organization's Exhibit B as management and general expenses.

Multiple Purpose Information Materials and Activities

Very frequently, requests for financial support incorporate information on an organization's activities or accomplishments. Often, such requests or appeals also contain information about health matters of benefit to the recipient.

In the development of the first edition of this book in 1964, the sponsoring organizations were highly concerned about the adverse impact on the credibility of nonprofit financial reporting resulting from several well publicized scandals of the day. Accordingly, a standard was then adopted which called for allocation to fund-raising of all multipurpose information expenses, other than the incremental direct costs of separate educational pieces: This was called the "primary purpose" cost allocation concept. While this resulted in an overstatement of fund-raising expenses, the magnitude of error was rarely material. However, with changing economic and social conditions, particularly with the expanded use of computer-based direct mail combined educational and fund-raising programs, a number of organizations found strict application of this standard to cause concern about overstatements of fund-raising expenses.

In 1987, the American Institute of Certified Public Accountants (AICPA) issued Statement of Position 87-2, "Accounting for Joint Costs of Informational Materials and Activities of Not-for-Profit Organizations that Include a Fund-raising Appeal." This document amended the AICPA's "Audits of Voluntary Health and Welfare Organizations" to clarify that a "primary purpose" approach to cost allocation was not in accordance with generally accepted accounting principles.

Although SOP 87-2 was an improvement over the "primary purpose" approach, there were still concerns regarding the clarity of the guidelines and its inconsistent application. Consequently, in March, 1998, the AICPA issued Statement of Position 98-2, "Accounting for Costs of Activities of Not-for-Profit Organizations and State and Local Governmental Entities That Include Fund Raising." The section below summarizes this new authoritative guidance, which is effective for financial statements for the years beginning on or after December 15, 1998.

Accounting for Costs of Joint Activities That Include a Fund-Raising Appeal

The standards to be followed when accounting for the costs of joint activities that include a fund-raising appeal are as follows:

All costs of joint activities that include a fund-raising appeal should be reported as fund-raising expense if it cannot be demonstrated that a program or management and general function has been conducted in conjunction with the appeal for funds. However, if all three criteria of purpose, audience and content are met (as defined below), then the cost of joint activities that are identifiable with a particular function should be charged to that function, and joint costs should be allocated between fund raising and the appropriate program or management and general function.

The following paragraphs detail the factors to consider in evaluating whether the purpose, audience and content criteria are met.

Purpose Criterion

The purpose criterion is met if the purpose of the joint activity includes accomplishing program or management and general functions. To accomplish program functions, the activity should call for specific action by the audience that will help accomplish the entity's mission. For example, assume that an entity's mission includes improving individuals' physical health. For that entity, motivating the audience to take specific action that will improve their physical health is a call for specific action by the audience that will help accomplish the entity's mission. An example of an activity that motivates the audience to take specific action that will improve their physical health is sending the audience a brochure that urges them to stop smoking and suggests specific methods, instructions, references and resources that may be used to stop smoking.

If the activity calls for specific action by the audience that will help accomplish the entity's mission, the following guidance should be considered, in the order listed, in determining whether the purpose criterion is met.

A) *Compensation Test*   The purpose criterion is not met if a majority of compensation or fees for any party's performance of any component of the discrete joint activity varies, based upon contributions raised for that discrete joint activity. For example, if a professional fund-raiser is paid a percentage of the receipts from a specific fund-raising event and that compensation represents the majority of the fees received, then the purpose criterion would not be met. The compensation test may apply to independent contractors or entity employees who conduct joint activities.

The compensation test is a negative test, that is, either the test is failed or you proceed to the next factor which is the similar function/similar medium test.

B) *Similar Function/Similar Medium Test*   The purpose criterion is met if a program or management and general activity that is similar to the program or management and general component of the activity being accounted for is conducted without the fund-raising component, using the same medium and on a scale that is similar to or greater than the scale on which it is conducted with the fund-raising component.

The similar function/similar medium test is a positive test in that it (1) results in passing the purpose criterion or (2) is not determinative of whether the purpose criterion is met. If the purpose criterion is not met based on the similar function/similar medium test, the other evidence below should be considered.

Other Evidence

a.   Evidence that the purpose criterion may be met includes

Measuring program results and accomplishments of the activity. The facts may indicate that the purpose criterion is met if the entity measures program results and accomplishments.

- *Medium*   The facts may indicate that the purpose criterion is met if the entity conducts the program or management and general component without a significant fund-raising component, in a different medium.

b. Evidence that the purpose criterion may not be met

- *Evaluation or compensation*   The facts may indicate that the purpose criterion is not met if (a) the evaluation of any party's performance of any component of the discrete joint activity varies, based on contributions raised for that discrete joint activity or (b) some, but less than a majority, of compensation or fees for any party's performance of any component of the discrete joint activity varies, based on contributions raised for that discrete joint activity.

c. *Evidence that the purpose criterion may be either met or not met*

- The entity places more weight on the accomplishment of one component over another. For example, more weight is placed on fund-raising than program activities.

- The qualifications, experience and range of services of those performing the joint activity are tilted toward one component over another.

- Tangible evidence of intent may provide an indication of the purpose of the activity. Such evidence includes entity's mission statement, minutes of meetings, plans or policies, internal management memos, etc.

All available evidence, both positive and negative, should be considered to determine whether, based on the weight of that evidence, the purpose criterion is met.

If the purpose criterion is met, then proceed to the audience criterion.

Audience Criterion

A rebuttable presumption exists that the audience criterion is not met if the audience includes prior donors or is otherwise selected based on its ability or likelihood to contribute to the entity. However, that presumption can be overcome if the audience is selected for one or more of the following reasons:

a. The audience's need to use (or reasonable potential for use of) the specific action called for by the program component of the joint activity.

b. The audience's ability to take specific action to assist the entity in meeting the goals of the program component of the joint activity.

c. The entity is required to direct the management and general component of the joint activity to the particular audience or the audience, has reasonable potential for use of the management and general component.

If the audience includes no prior donors and is not selected based on its ability to contribute, the audience criterion is met if the audience is selected for any of the three reasons stated in the paragraph above.

Content Criterion

The content criterion is met if the activity supports program or management and general functions as follows:

- (Program) The activity calls for specific action by the recipient to help accomplish the entity's mission. If the need for and benefits of the action are not clearly evident, information describing the action and explaining the need for and benefits of the action is provided.

- (Management and General) The joint activity fulfills one or more of the entity's management and general responsibilities through a component of the joint activity.

Allocation Methods

The cost allocation methodology should be rational and systematic, it should result in an allocation of joint costs that is reasonable, and it should be applied consistently given similar facts and circumstances.

In applying these concepts to the activities of a voluntary health or welfare agency, all of the circumstances surrounding the joint activity must be considered, and a conclusion reached based on facts. Once it has been determined that a bona fide joint activity has been conducted, joint costs should be allocated equitably to their respective functions.

The applications of normal cost accounting techniques will result in allocations which fairly reflect the purposes for which the activity was conducted. Voluntary health and welfare organizations have long experience with allocating the costs of salaries, rent, telephone and other expenses to program, fund-raising, and management and general through the use of such techniques as estimates of space usage, time reports and so forth.

In the case of joint activities, the joint costs should be allocated based on the degree to which the cost were incurred for the function to which they are allocated. Only joint costs are to be allocated. Expenses which are directly identifiable with fund-raising or another function should be charged directly to that function.

REMINDER: If the joint activity does not meet all three criteria (purpose, audience and content) but includes a fund-raising appeal, all costs will be charged to fund-raising, including the costs which in other circumstances would be considered program costs.

Incidental Activities

If incidental activities are conducted along with a primary activity, and the criteria for allocation are met, joint costs may, but do not have to be, allocated to incidental activities.

Disclosures

Entities that allocate joint costs should disclose the following in their financial statements:

a. The types of activities for which joint costs have been incurred.

b. A statement that such costs have been allocated.

c. The total amount allocated during the period and the portion allocated to each functional expense category.

SOP 98-2 encourages, but does not require that the amount of joint costs for each kind of joint activity be disclosed.

[Please see Appendix 5 for examples showing application of joint cost principles.]

Awards and Grants

Functional expense accounting and reporting by voluntary organizations require that special attention be given to awards and grants that organizations make to individuals and other organizations for a variety of purposes. The latter frequently include grants to individuals and to universities and other institutions unrelated to an organization. Many organizations also voluntarily make special research or other program grants to national affiliates, apart from and in addition to prescribed support quotas or percentages of local-national campaign proceeds they remit to the nationals.

The standard treatment of awards and grants requires that organizations account for them according to their ultimate purpose. Grants for research, for special studies and for other projects that are natural extensions of one of an organization's service programs, or consistent with a program purpose, should be reported as part of those program services expenses. In the case of payments to affiliated organizations, however, only payments that are voluntary on the part of an organization, subject to its own discretion and intended for specific service programs, may be reported as awards or grants in a functional category. (For treatment of other payments to affiliated organizations, see page 86.)

Organizations that report awards and grants as program services expenses must disclose, parenthetically or otherwise, awards and grants for each program category made to affiliated organizations, and the amount made to others. (See Exhibit C.)

Organizations that make grants to others should record grants as expenses and liabilities at the time recipients are entitled to them. That normally occurs when the grantee is notified; although some organizations recognize grant liabilities at the time of board approval. Some grants stipulate that payments are to be made over a period of several years. Grants payable in future periods, with donor-imposed conditions, should be recognized as liabilities if the likelihood of not meeting the condition is remote. The transaction must be recorded at discounted present value. The organization should look at prior grant activity to assess whether the likelihood of not meeting the condition is remote. When practical, refunds and cancellations of prior-year grants should be offset against current grant expense and the amount disclosed.

Object Categories in Statement of Functional Expenses

Chapter 3 includes a general discussion of the purpose and format of Exhibit C, while a discussion of methods of allocating expenses among an organization's program and supporting service functions will be found in Appendix 1. The expenses to be included in each object classification listed on each line of Exhibit C are explained and illustrated below.

Organizations may use additional categories, may combine two or more categories into one, or may divide a category into two or more categories, if this is considered desirable for clear financial presentation, without obscuring necessary detail. The categories used should be consistent over time, and disclosure should be made of the nature of significant differences from the illustrated categories.

Salaries

Intended for: Salaries and wages earned by an organization's regular employees (full or part-time) and by temporary employees, including office temporaries, other than consultants and other persons engaged on an individual contract basis.

Illustrations:

- Executive salaries

- Professional staff salaries

- Clerical salaries

- Maintenance employees' wages

- Bonus or incentive payments

- Vacation and other compensated absences

Note: Individual organizations may subdivide this account— e.g., to show professional salaries separate from clerical and maintenance salaries and wages—as long as they show the totals of all salaries and wages opposite this caption on Exhibit C.

Employee Benefits

Intended for: Amounts paid and accrued by an organization under its own or other private employee health and retirement benefit plans, including voluntary employee termination or retirement payments outside a formal plan.

Illustrations:

- Accident insurance premiums or cost reimbursement

- Medical and hospital plan premiums or cost reimbursement

- Pension or retirement plan contributions

- Matching or other contributions to employee savings or similar plans

- Other benefits (holiday gifts, use of recreational facilities, prepaid legal plan, etc.)

Payroll Taxes, Etc.

Intended for: Social Security taxes and compensation insurance premiums, payable by employers under federal, state or local laws.

Illustrations:

- F.I.C.A. payments (employer's share)

- Unemployment insurance premiums

- Worker's compensation insurance

- Mandatory disability insurance premiums

Professional and Other Contract Service Fees

Intended for: Fees and expenses of professional practitioners and consultants who are not employees of the reporting organization and are engaged as independent contractors for specified services on a fee or other individual contract basis.

Illustrations:

- Legal fees

- Auditing and accounting fees and expenses

- Contract payments to independent professional consultants

- Fund-raising counsel fees

- Actuarial fees

- Data processing services (outside vendor)

- Investment management fees (not commissions on transactions)

- Contracted software development

- Media production costs

Supplies

Intended for: Costs of materials, appliances and other supplies used by an organization.

Illustrations:

- Medicines and drugs

- Prosthetic appliances

- Recreational and crafts materials

- Food and beverages

- Laundry, linen and housekeeping materials

- Stationery, typing, accounting and other office materials

- Paper, ink, film and duplicating materials

Telephone

Intended for: All telephone, telecommunications and similar expenses.

Postage and Shipping

Intended for: Postage, parcel post, express mail, trucking and other delivery expenses, including shipping materials.

Occupancy

Intended for: All costs arising from an organization's occupancy and use of owned or leased land, buildings and offices. This excludes costs associated with housing but which are reported in other object categories—e.g., salaries, depreciation on buildings, insurance.

Illustrations:

- Office rent

- Electricity, heat and other utilities

- Janitorial and other maintenance services under contract

- Building and grounds maintenance supplies

Interest Expense

Intended for: Interest incurred on mortgage notes, capitalized equipment leases, and other short- or long-term debt.

Rental and Maintenance of Equipment

Intended for: Cost of renting and maintaining equipment (such as computers and copiers), including program and other equipment. The rental and maintenance of automotive vehicles should be included in travel/transportation.

Printing and Publications

Intended for: Costs of printing, commercial artists and suppliers for plates, advertising, art work, proofs, photographs and other costs of house organs, leaflets, films and other information materials, including the cost of purchased publications, technical journals, books, pamphlets and monographs.

Travel and Transportation

Intended for: Expenses of travel and transportation for staff and volunteers of the reporting organization. Travel costs related to conferences can be included in the conferences category below.

Illustrations:

- Transportation fees, mileage allowances, hotel, meals and incidental expenses

- Local bus and taxicab fares

- Automobile expenses of operating organization-owned or leased vehicles used for programs or general purposes, except insurance

- Allowances for use of employees' or volunteers' automobiles on business for organization

Conferences, Conventions and Meetings

Intended for: Expenses of conducting or attending meetings related to an organization's activities, other than travel costs which should be included in the preceding category.

Illustrations:

- Meeting space and equipment rentals

- Meeting program, notices, badges and related printing costs

- Cost of organized meals

- Speakers' honorariums and expenses

- Conference and convention registration fees for organization staff participants

Specific Assistance to Individuals

Intended for: The cost to the reporting organization of assistance or services for a particular client or patient, including assistance rendered by others at the expense of the reporting organization.

Illustrations:

- Medical, dental and hospital fees and charges

- Children's board

- Homemaker services

- Client and patient travel

- Food, shelter and clothing

- Individual camperships

Note: This category is also designed to include materials and appliances furnished by the reporting organization when purchased for or identifiable with a particular client or patient.

Membership Dues

Intended for: Amounts paid or payable for bona fide membership in other organizations which provide, in return, benefits such as regular services, publications, materials, etc.

Note: This category covers payments of the type that are to be reported as other revenue by receiving health and welfare organizations. For example, national organizations include such amounts received in assessments and dues from local member units. (See Chapter 4.) Payments that do not procure, for the paying organization, general membership benefits, as described in Chapter 4, should be reported as contributions, as described in the sections on awards, grants and payments to affiliated organizations earlier in this chapter.

Awards and Grants

Intended for: Amount paid or committed to individuals or organizations for support of research, fellowship, scholarship and other health or welfare programs. Amounts paid to affiliated organizations should be reported separately from amounts paid to others. (See Exhibit C.)

Illustrations:

- Grants to research institutions

- Graduate fellowships

- Trainee scholarships

- Allowances for travel and equipment under particular awards or grants

- Contributions or grants which are formula-based or prescribed payments by an organization in support of an affiliate should not be shown opposite this caption (See the section on payments to affiliated organizations in this chapter.)

Insurance

Intended for: All costs of insurance except employee benefits or other payroll-related insurance (worker's compensation, disability, unemployment). Should include property insurance, general liability, professional liability (e.g., malpractice), fidelity bonds, directors' and officers' liability, automobile and other vehicles, meeting cancellation, business interruption insurance. (Should not include insurance provided to beneficiaries of an organization's programs—included with Specific Assistance to Individuals.)

Other Expenses

This classification needs no explanation, but a word of caution may be appropriate. If the expenses of an organization have been properly classified, very little should usually remain to be shown as other.

Depreciation or Amortization

Intended for: Allocation of the cost, or other carrying value, of physical assets over their estimated useful lives. Provision for depreciation or amortization is an accounting process intended to spread the cost of such assets over the period of time their use benefits the program or supporting activities of the organization; it should not be viewed as a means of funding their replacement.

Illustrations:

- Depreciation—equipment.

- Amortization—leasehold improvements and capital leases

- Depreciation—automotive equipment

- Depreciation—buildings

Contributed Goods and Services

Intended for: All materials and services volunteered in order to further the mission of the organization. These goods and services should be allocated to the appropriate functional category but they may be kept as a separate natural expense class.

Illustration:

- Free legal services

- Free peer review of grants

- Free construction help

- Free TV or radio ads

- Free printing

Reporting of Assets, Liabilities and Net Assets

A nnual reporting to the public is incomplete if confined to an organization's operating statements, as seen in Exhibits B, C, and D in Chapter 8. The public is also entitled to know the nature and carrying values of all significant assets an organization owns, and of debts it owes, and to see that the organization recognizes necessary distinctions by class that must be accounted for separately, as discussed in Chapter 2. To present this further evidence of their stewardship of the public's support, SFAS 117 requires that not-for-profit organizations include a balance sheet in their annual published financial statements. Voluntary health and welfare organizations should present their balance sheet conforming in content and format, to the extent appropriate for each organization, to Exhibit A, Chapter 8. (As noted earlier, SFAS 117 does not require that any particular title be used, so organizations may choose to name this statement the Statement of Assets and Liabilities, Statement of Financial Position or another meaningful title.)

The most conspicuous difference between Exhibit A and the balance sheets commonly used by businesses is that Exhibit A presents the organization's net assets (equity) in not one, but three pieces—one for each of the organization's classes of net assets: unrestricted, temporarily restricted, permanently restricted. Each net asset amount is the result of changes in net assets related to that class. Segregation, in a balance sheet, of at least the net assets of each class is essential to demonstrate that the organization has honored restrictions attached to gifts by particular donors—e.g., to show that contributions for permanent endowment have been accounted for separately, and not included in accounts of resources available for unrestricted purposes.

Presentation of Classes of Net Assets

SFAS 117 requires only the total column, as long as net assets by class are presented, normally on separate lines within the net assets section as shown. For many organizations, especially those which have only minor amounts of restricted net assets, the total column alone will provide adequate information to readers. Presentation of additional columns, showing segregation of assets and liabilities, is permitted if desired, but not required, such as when the assets of separate classes are not interchangeable. Such additional columns may present the classes of net assets, individual funds or fund groups (e.g., operating funds, plant funds, endowment funds), or separate operational units of the organization (e.g., a day care center, a senior citizens center). Each organization should choose the format which it considers most meaningful to the readers of its financial statements, but the format and terminology shown in Exhibit A (with or without the additional columns) is considered appropriate and is recommended.

Assets held by an outside trustee, in trust for the benefit of an organization, generate investment income that is remitted periodically to the organization. Historically, such assets have not been included in organizations' balance sheets. However, where such trusts are irrevocable and the organization is guaranteed a defined future stream of income, the essence of the arrangement is that of a promise to give (pledge) of the future income, to be earned by the trust. Under SFAS 116, unconditional pledges (discussed further below) are reported as assets and restricted revenue when notification of the pledge is received. Thus, when an organization is notified of the creation of such a third-party trust, the organization should record the amount of the pledge as a receivable and as revenue. Since the organization will never obtain access to the principal amount of such a trust, the revenue should be recorded in the permanently restricted class of net assets. The value to be recorded should be the present value of the future cash flows (income) expected to be received, which will, in most cases, equal the current fair value of the trust assets. The facts of the trust arrangement, to the extent they are ascertainable, should be disclosed in a note accompanying the organization's financial statements.

The reader's understanding of financial statements published by similar organizations will be improved by organizations' adherence to uniform terminology. To the extent possible, voluntary health and welfare organizations should conform their balance sheet account titles and content to those presented in Exhibit A and described below. Neither Exhibit A nor the following discussions purport, however, to be all-inclusive; individual organizations should supplement or expand the accounts described here for adequate disclosure of particular assets or liabilities. On the other hand, some accounts may not be required. Organizations may select those accounts for reporting that reflect their particular assets, liabilities and net assets. An account may be combined with another account of a similar type if the amount in one of the accounts alone is insignificant.

Cash and Cash Equivalents

Assets are normally listed in a balance sheet with the most liquid items shown first. Thus cash, whose liquidity is usually absolute, should be the first caption in a balance sheet. This item should include all cash actually held by an organization. Cash on deposit in checking accounts, deposits in transit, change funds and petty cash funds held for operating purposes may properly be combined. The portion of cash which is deposited in interest-bearing accounts such as N.O.W. accounts or savings accounts (including money market accounts) should be disclosed on the statement or in a footnote. Cash held by a custodian as part of a managed investment account may be included with the investments on the balance sheet, or it may be included with other cash. Disclosure should be made of cash amounts which may not be readily available, such as those held in an escrow account.

An item should not be recorded as cash until the money is actually received by an organization. It is improper, for example, to show receivables as cash prior to the date of their actual collection.

Short-term Investments

Short-term investments may, because of their liquidity, appear as a separate caption after cash, or they may be included with cash, or, if preferred, be included with long-term investments. They represent temporary investments of cash not immediately required. Examples are United States Treasury bills, certificates of deposit, bankers acceptances, repurchase agreements, and commercial paper. They are usually quickly convertible into cash, and their maturities may range anywhere from a few days to a year. It should be recognized, however, that the distinction between whether a particular investment is reported as short-term or noncurrent is not the nature of the investment, but rather the intention of the organization with regard to the timing of its eventual conversion into cash.

Accounts Receivable

For consistency with accrual accounting as the recognized basis for public financial reporting by voluntary health and welfare organizations, uncollected accounts receivable should be shown in their balance sheet. Accounts receivable from all sources other than contributors (pledges—see next section) are included in the accounts receivable section. These receivables frequently result from an organization's program services. They may also arise through operation of revenue-producing activities, such as sales of materials or publications. Reimbursements due from affiliates, claims against vendors, accrued investment income, and advances to staff members are other receivables that may be sufficiently important to require separate disclosure in an organization's balance sheet.

An organization should show in the balance sheet, or in a footnote, the nature and amounts of significant individual classes of accounts receivable included in the total shown—e.g., clients or customers, government agencies, etc. In addition, significant receivables from related parties such as employees, volunteers, affiliated organizations, etc., should be presented separately or otherwise disclosed.

Accounts receivable should be analyzed as to the likelihood of their being collected in full. Any allowance for uncollectible accounts that is considered necessary, on the basis of the analysis, should be shown as a deduction from the related receivable in the balance sheet. The change in the allowance for the year (whether an increase or decrease) is included in the appropriate expense category for the year reported in Exhibit B.

Pledges (Promises to Give) Receivable

A frequently raised question about financial reporting to the public is related to the problems of accounting for pledges receivable. Some have argued that including these is impractical because it requires what they believe are questionable estimates as to the amounts that may be collected, and because voluntary organizations usually will not take legal action to enforce collection of pledges.

For many voluntary health and welfare organizations, however, contributions by way of pledges are too important to be overlooked. For example, many federated fund-raising organizations encourage contributors to make pledges rather than cash contributions and to pay them by regular payroll deductions or installment payments. Building fund drives or other campaigns of voluntary organizations also often receive large grants that are payable in installments. Nor can an organization ignore a pledge from a regular contributor simply because payment is deferred until the next year. In other words, any organization has an obligation to report, in its financial statements, significant pledges that are expected to be collected. Footnotes should include a table indicating the total amount of pledges due to be collected in less than one year, one to five years, and over five years, and related discount and allowance.

SFAS 116 requires organizations to record unconditional promises to give (essentially the same as pledges; this book will continue to use the more familiar term) for which there is verifiable evidence of their existence. SFAS 116 also requires that pledges due after one year be discounted to present value to reflect the time value of money. A pledge of $1,000 due today is worth more than $1,000 due in five years. Each year, the present value of the pledge increases to reflect the fact that collection of the full $1,000 is now going to happen sooner. Further discussion of discounting is found in Accounting Principles Board Opinion 21. SFAS 116 makes one change from APB 21: the accretion of discounted pledges to their ultimate collection value is reported as contribution income, not interest income.

If total omission of significant pledges from an entity's financial statements is indefensible, mechanical reporting of all pledges received by an organization is no more acceptable. Before pledges may properly be included in support and revenue and in an organization's balance sheet, they must be evaluated as to the existence of any conditions which must be fulfilled before payment is due, and for the likelihood of payment.

Conditional pledges are those for which the right of collection does not exist until after the occurrence of some uncertain future event specified by the donor. Examples of conditions include: the meeting of the terms of a challenge grant, the occurrence of a natural disaster, receiving approval of a governmental body to conduct some activity, future financial ability of the pledgor to make payments under the pledge. Conditional pledges are not recorded until the specified event occurs, at which time the pledge becomes unconditional. The amount of conditional pledges received by the entity but not recorded should be disclosed in a footnote. Promises to give are distinguished from statements of intention to give, which are not promises at all. Disclosure of intentions to give is not required.

With experience and a systematic approach, evaluation of the likelihood of payment can become reasonably accurate. Organizations can usually identify certain pledges as unlikely ever to be paid, others as quite reliable. One practical way to evaluate pledges still unpaid is to "age" them—to group them according to the time which has passed since they were to have been paid. Groups might be established for those not yet due, those up to thirty days old, thirty to sixty days old, sixty to ninety days old, etc. With experience, a reasonable factor usually can be developed for the percentage of each group that probably will be collected. Use of the aging technique requires only that an organization keep records of payments on pledges to which it can refer as a basis for estimating the probable yield of future pledges of different ages and types. Another way to evaluate pledges, which might be used by United Ways and federated fund-raising organizations that receive pledges payable through payroll deduction, is to analyze historical trends of collection by company, industry, or employee group.

In Exhibit B, amounts unconditionally pledged are reported as public support in the year the pledge is received or becomes unconditional. The amount recorded is reduced for the present value discount applicable to new pledges, increased for the accretion of the discount on pledges recorded in prior years, and is reported net of a deduction for amounts related to new pledges recorded that year that are estimated to prove uncollectible. The amounts to be shown as pledges receivable in Exhibit A, on the other hand, are totals, again after allowing for the discount and for estimated uncollectible amounts, of all pledges unpaid at the balance sheet date. These include not only pledges received in the current year, but also amounts receivable from years prior to the current year. The purely voluntary character of pledges, in most instances, makes it necessary that they be presented separately from other receivables.

Such reporting of pledges in an organization's balance sheet clearly requires that it, at least annually, re-evaluate its prior years' receivables with particular care and possibly write off some, and change allowances for uncollectibility with respect to others. Any resulting adjustments should be reported as administrative expenses (for unrestricted pledges) or losses (for restricted pledges) in the current year Exhibit B. If uncollected pledges are carefully evaluated and included in each year's Balance Sheet at realistic values, subsequent years' adjustments and write-offs should not be significant.

Many pledges are made in one year but intended to be paid in a subsequent year or years. Prior to the adoption of SFAS 116, such pledges were reported as deferred income (support and revenue designated for future periods) in the year-end balance sheet. SFAS 116 requires all unconditional pledges to be reported in the same way as other contributions: that is, as revenue in the year received, regardless of when payment is expected. (The expected timing of payment is reflected in the present value discount.) Most pledges result in increases in the temporarily restricted class of net assets where they remain until the period of expected collection, at which time they are reclassified to the unrestricted class. Exceptions would be pledges which are further restricted for some operating or endowment purpose. Pledges for permanent endowment would be reported in the permanently restricted class of net assets; pledges for specific operating purposes would remain in the temporarily restricted class until the purpose is satisfied; pledges specified for unrestricted use in the current period would be reported in the unrestricted class.

Inventory

The inventory category refers to materials and goods purchased or manufactured by, or donated to, an organization, and held to be sold, either to affiliated or other organizations or to the public, or to be used in operations in some future period. (Items to be used rather than sold could also be called prepaid expenses.) These items are assets at the date of the Balance Sheet, because they represent something of determinable value, are on hand and have not yet been distributed or used. As to the future, they represent either expenses which will be applied to future operations or items for sale for which an organization will later collect cash. The range of items for possible reporting in this asset classification may include bulletins and literature on hand that can be used in the future—e.g., in fund-raising activities—food to be used in a summer camp, supplies for camping activities or for the office, insignia, printed lesson material, medicines and materials to be distributed to welfare recipients or to other organizations in connection with organization programs. They should be valued and presented in an organization's Balance Sheet, however, only if they can be sold, or to the extent that they can be expected to be used in some future program or supporting activity of the organization. Items which have been donated may be included in this caption, if they meet the above requirement, to the extent of the values at which they have been recorded as contributions, as discussed below.

Inventory should be recorded on the balance sheet at the lower of: (1) actual cost, (2) the amount for which they are to be sold in the case of items for sale, or (3) in the case of material to be used in future operations, the value they still have for the organization's purposes.

It sometimes becomes necessary to make adjustments in amounts of inventory because items held have lost their value. This may occur because of spoilage or damage, or because of obsolescence resulting from a change in program. Materials for fund-raising purposes are such an example. If these materials are procured in advance for a campaign and are being held for distribution at the time of the statement, they should be shown as inventory. If they are dated or otherwise unusable for subsequent campaigns, however, they should not be included in inventory. Deteriorated or unusable materials should be written off by charging the cost to the function for which they were originally acquired.

Prepaid Expenses and Deferred Charges

To provide comparable and consistent reporting of support, revenue and expenses, it may be necessary to make accounting adjustments to carry forward, or defer to the following year, expense prepayments of a material amount—e.g., insurance—applicable to future years, or expenses properly related to a future year's activities, such as advance expenses for the following year's program activities. These items are to be carried in the Balance Sheet until the period for which they are proper expenses.

Only those fund-raising expenses specifically identifiable with fund-raising efforts to be undertaken in future years may be deferred. No portion of expenses related to current fund-raising efforts may be deferred, even though some of the resulting contributions may not be received until future years. Certain advertising (but not fund-raising) costs may also be deferred (under AICPA SOP 93-7) if the purpose of the advertising is to solicit direct responses from customers or clients which can be directly related to the advertising, and if it can be shown that the deferred costs will be recovered out of future net cash inflows resulting from the advertising.

Noncurrent Investments

This investment caption is used to report investments intended to be held for periods of time longer than a year for income-producing purposes. As contrasted with short-term, the purpose of noncurrent investments is not to seek early recovery of principal, but to obtain continuing investment income and/or capital appreciation.

Exhibit A reflects two groups of long-term investments. The first is board-designated, noncurrent investments within the unrestricted class of net assets, which the governing board may use at its own discretion. The second is investments related to the net assets of the permanently restricted endowment fund which are restricted by donors and subject to the terms of the gifts and/or legacies.

Noncurrent investments might consist of government bonds, corporate stocks and bonds or even real estate. Note that this caption can also include investments maturing in a short time if there is the intention and ability to reinvest the proceeds. Where the amounts of investments are significant, the major types of investments are common stocks, preferred stocks, corporate bonds, government bonds, real estate, mortgages, etc.

If organization owns such a large percentage of the stock of one company that the company is effectively controlled by the organization, accounting on the equity method or full consolidation is appropriate. Guidance for accounting for such investments is in AICPA SOP 94-3, which requires that companies in which an organization holds majority voting ownership must be consolidated, and those in which the percentage of ownership is short of a majority, but still large enough that the organization has significant influence, should be carried on the equity method.

Additional discussion of affiliated organizations is in Chapter 7.

Investments purchased by voluntary health and welfare organizations should be initially recorded at cost, which includes brokerage, taxes and other charges directly applicable to the purchase. Securities donated to the organization should be recorded at their fair market value at the date of the gift (if the security is sold very shortly after receipt, the value is best measured by the net proceeds received). In the year-end balance sheet, equity securities with a readily determinable fair value and all debt securities in the investment portfolio should be marked to current fair market value in accordance with SFAS 124. The change (whether positive or negative) in unrealized appreciation (or depreciation) should be reported as a gain or loss in the appropriate class of net assets, as discussed in Chapter 4, in the Statement of Activities. Other investments should be valued as discussed in Paragraph 8.28 (2) of the AICPA audit guide.

Fixed Assets and Depreciation

The stewardship and reporting responsibility of voluntary organizations extends to land, buildings and equipment (whether purchased, donated or financed by contributors), no less than to cash and other assets. Contributors whose donations have been used to acquire property are entitled to know what their dollars have bought, and readers of the financial statements are entitled to see in the balance sheet all important assets for which management is responsible.

Voluntary organizations usually acquire items of property and equipment either by purchase or by gift. Fixed assets may be held for use (service potential), for investment or for sale.

Inextricably involved with fixed assets is the question of depreciation of these assets. The following sections describe accounting for the acquisition, depreciation and replacement of fixed assets by voluntary health and welfare organizations.

Organizations should account for and report separately fixed assets held for investment or sale, and those held for use. Assets held for investment or sale should be included in the class of net assets appropriate to any donor-imposed restrictions on their use. (See Chapter 4 for a discussion of alternatives for reporting donated fixed assets.) If amounts of restricted assets are significant, they should be separately disclosed. Amounts reported on the balance sheet should be as discussed above under noncurrent investments.

Many organizations will wish to maintain a separate land, building and equipment fund in the organization's accounting records to record transactions relating to assets, depreciation, mortgages, other liabilities and net assets involving fixed assets held for use by an organization, and for contributions restricted by donors for the acquisition or construction of fixed assets for use. "Held for use" are the key words. No other assets (fixed or otherwise) or liabilities should be carried in this fund unless they relate to this purpose. Such a fund may be shown separately on the balance sheet, within the appropriate class(es) of net assets if the organization desires. Since the resources used to acquire fixed assets often are a combination of unrestricted resources and resources restricted for the purchase of fixed assets, it may not be clear whether proceeds from later sale of assets purchased with restricted amounts continue to bear the original donor restrictions. Resolution of this issue is a legal matter.

An organization's balance sheet, or the notes thereto, should normally show separate amounts for land, for buildings (and equipment built into them) and for furniture, furnishings and office equipment which are owned, or are rented under leases which are capital leases. Even so-called "fixed" assets exhibit wide differences in real value; land has lasting value, while automobiles, for instance, become uneconomical to operate in a relatively short time. Segregation of an organization's fixed asset values into types, as indicated above, assists readers of its balance sheet to understand the relative significance of values shown for different classes of property. The particular assets owned by a given organization may call either for a classification different from that shown in Exhibit A—e.g., canoes that represent a major equipment category of an organization camp—or for subdivision of one of the above classifications. The objective sought in classifying an organization's fixed assets should be to group assets similar in nature.

Purchased fixed assets should be recorded at actual cost and donated assets at their fair market value at the date of the gift. Actual cost may include an agent's fees, acquisition costs, freight, installation and sales taxes, and other costs incurred in addition to the asset cost. Cost of assets constructed by volunteer labor will include an amount representing the value of the time of the volunteers, as discussed in Chapter 4 under donated services of volunteers. In the absence of adequate cost records, appraisals of historical cost or market value at date of the gift are acceptable for initial valuation for financial reporting purposes. If assets which are constructed for the organization are financed with borrowed money, it may be necessary to capitalize interest incurred during construction on the borrowing as part of the cost of the assets and to disclose in the notes the policy and the amount of interest capitalized.

Depreciation of fixed assets held for use should be included as an element of expenses in the appropriate categories in the statement of functional expenses, and also in the unrestricted class in the statement of activity. Fixed assets should be reported net on the balance sheet with accumulated depreciation disclosed on the statement or in a footnote.

An entity that desires to set aside or appropriate funds for self-financing or fixed asset replacement may do so by board action. It should report the appropriation under the "designated by the governing board" classification in the unrestricted net asset section of the balance sheet. (See also the discussion of reserves and appropriations in Chapter 2.)

Methods of valuing fixed assets, depreciable lives and methods of computing depreciation should be disclosed.

The principle that voluntary organizations report the values of the fixed assets they own in their balance sheets raises a number of practical accounting questions. What are the "fixed assets"? How far are voluntary organizations expected to go in attempting to inventory, set up detailed records for, and value items of equipment? Are voluntary organizations expected to show in their own balance sheets land and buildings that they occupy and use but that are owned by another organization (as in the case, for instance, with many church-sponsored organizations)? On what basis are organizations expected to value assets acquired over a period of years for which no cost records are available? How are donated items of property and equipment to be valued? Although these last two questions have been previously answered to some extent, more attention will be given to them in the following discussion.

Voluntary organizations should not include in their balance sheet values for land, buildings and equipment they occupy and use, but which are owned by another organization, except as discussed in the following paragraph. Organizations so favored should disclose the facts, however, in a note to their financial statements—e.g.: "The accompanying financial statements do not reflect the value of the land and buildings occupied by the organization, as these are recorded in the name of the Bishop of the Diocese of [Arlington]." However, as was discussed in Chapter 4, the rental value of contributed space should be reported both as a contribution and as an expense to reflect occupancy.

However, if an organization occupies real property owned by a private owner or a governmental unit, and the owner has agreed that the organization shall have use of the property for an indefinite period, the organization may have an unconditional promise to give, which amounts to a capital lease on the property thus the organization may need to include the property on its balance sheet. Similarly, an organization may have acquired fixed assets with money from a grant in which the grantor retains a reversionary interest in the property at the end of the grant period. In many such situations, the grantor, in fact, typically lets the organization retain the property. Such property should also be included on the organization's balance sheet if it is likely that the organization will, in fact, retain the property. In both situations, full disclosure of the circumstances surrounding the property should be made.

Small items of office equipment, minor furnishings, hand tools and the like, on the other hand, are generally too numerous and of too little individual value to warrant the effort to inventory and value them. An arbitrary minimum value (except for groups of items substantial in amount) might be established below which individual items or groups of items would not be capitalized, but would be reported as expenses when acquired. This minimum value will vary based on the size of the organization.

Donated Land, Buildings and Equipment

As indicated, the standards discussed previously for accounting for land, buildings and equipment apply to donated as well as to purchased property. It is recognized, nonetheless, that organizations occasionally receive donations of furnishings, furniture and other items for which they have little need, or which are of much finer quality than they would normally acquire. If the organization intends to dispose of the items, they should be recorded in the unrestricted class at their fair value at the date of the gift. If the organization intends to use the items, or if the donor has restricted the gift in such a way that the organization cannot dispose of it, then the value should be a figure that realistically reflects the value of the items to the organization. Thus an unusually expensive donation would be adjusted to its "utility" value. It may be necessary to explain the accounting treatment in a note to the organization's financial statements, depending on materiality.

Accounts Payable and Accrued Expenses

Two types of "unpaid" items need to be recognized, at least in an organization's year-end accounting. The first consists of "bills," invoices for individual purchases or statements summarizing a month's transactions—e.g., cleaning services, electricity, telephone charges. These are referred to as "accounts payable." The second group encompasses expenses that accumulate, or accrue, to some extent automatically, with the passage of time. Rent, salaries (and related fringe benefits such as payroll taxes, vacation pay and post-employment benefits such as pensions, medical insurance and severance pay), property taxes and mortgage interest payments are examples. "Accrued expenses" is the term used to describe liabilities of this type. Other liabilities requiring recognition, if they exist, in an organization's balance sheet may include such debts as bank loans or loans from an affiliated organization, and amounts due under capital leases. Payables would also include grants payable to others discounted to present value as discussed in Chapter 5. Footnote disclosure should be made which will allow readers to be aware of the approximate maturity of grants and other contributions payable. This can be accomplished by listing the amount payable in one year, between one and five years, and over five years.

Revenue Designated for Future Periods (Refundable Advances)

This is a deferred revenue caption under which an organization should group, with details appropriate to the magnitude and types of revenue involved, items such as prepaid fees received for goods or services to be furnished in future periods, governmental fees or grants that are equivalent to fees for purchases of goods or services, membership dues and other fees. It should not be used to accumulate "reserves" or contingency appropriations, which would impair comparability of balance sheets and be misleading to contributors.

Prior to adoption of SFAS 116, this section would have included contributions (including contributions to capital campaigns) and other support that contributors or grantors have designated as payable for or applicable to a future year. Under SFAS 116, this is no longer appropriate; all such contributions are recorded as revenue upon receipt of a gift or unconditional pledge, as discussed in Chapter 5.

Similarly, the unspent portion of gifts or other revenue restricted by donors and grantors for specific purposes, but without a restriction as to time period of use, should not be recorded as deferred revenue. All such revenue should be recorded as revenue when the organization is entitled to receive payment. The unspent portion will then be included in the net asset amount of the temporarily restricted class of net assets.

Interclass (or Interfund) Receivables and Payables

Interclass/fund accounts will be required if an organization makes interclass/fund loans. Other interclass/fund accounts may arise from the common and acceptable practice of initially recording transactions, affecting any of an organization's accounts, in the unrestricted class of net assets. Materials chargeable to a fund restricted to support of research, for instance, might be paid for from a general bank account (maintained for more than one fund) and be charged, initially, to an account of the unrestricted fund or class. Afterwards, an entry would be made in the latter fund crediting the account and charging the expenses for bookkeeping purposes to the appropriate account for research in the current restricted fund (even though, for financial reporting purposes, as discussed in Chapter 5, the expense is reported in the unrestricted class.)

For annual public reporting purposes, it is desirable that such interclass/fund accounts be eliminated as far as practicable—i.e., as indicated in the above illustration—by a bookkeeping entry or, where separate bank accounts are maintained for each fund, by an actual cash transfer restoring the amount paid for the supplies to the current unrestricted fund cash balance and reducing the research fund cash. The advantage gained in eliminating interclass/fund accounts is that individual class balance sheets will then show the actual cash balances available to meet their respective external liabilities and future expenses.

If it becomes evident that contemplated sources of money for repayment of interclass/fund receivables will not be available in the foreseeable future, such loans should be considered permanent, and should be recorded as transfers, by charging the lending funds, crediting the borrowing funds, and eliminating the interclass/fund balances.

There may be legal prohibitions against lending such funds and against recording such transfers. If so, appropriate disclosure should be made. Material interclass/fund borrowings should be disclosed when restricted amounts have been loaned or when the liquidity of either class/fund is in question.

When the columnar format (Exhibit A) is used, interclass/ fund balances should be presented entirely on one line in the asset section, adding across to zero (the class/fund which shows the payable will report it as a negative number) to avoid overstating the aggregate assets and liabilities of the entity as a whole.

Other Assets and Liabilities

Voluntary health and welfare organizations vary so widely in size, programs and financing that it is impractical to attempt to devise an all-inclusive classification of balance sheet accounts for them. Only the major classes of assets and liabilities with which most voluntary organizations will have to deal in seeking to achieve uniform public financial reporting have been considered here. Circumstances of individual organizations may, for example, require accounting for mortgage obligations, long-term notes payable or other assets and liabilities substantially identical with those of commercial entities.

SFAS 117 requires that organizations include in their balance sheets information about the liquidity of their assets and liabilities. This may be accomplished in any of several ways. The most common is to report the various assets and liabilities in order of liquidity, with the most liquid assets (ease of conversion into cash) and liabilities (closest time that payment will be required) being reported nearer the top of the balance sheet.

Many organizations have only unrestricted net assets. Those organizations may wish to classify their assets as current, fixed or other long-term assets, and their liabilities as current or long-term. To be classified as "current," the assets generally should be realizable and the liabilities payable within a normal operating cycle. However, if there is no normal operating cycle or the operating cycle is less than one year, all assets expected to be converted to cash and cash equivalents within one year, and all liabilities to be liquidated within one year, should be classified as current.

Organizations which have both unrestricted and restricted net assets and which wish to present a fully disaggregated balance sheet, as discussed above, may find that the net asset classifications themselves adequately disclose the current and long-term nature of the related assets and liabilities. If not, a classified balance sheet may be presented, or information about liquidity may be presented in footnotes.

Classified Balance Sheet

Appropriations—Board-Designated Amounts

Some nonprofit organizations, on occasion, create general "reserves" or make general appropriations from balances of unrestricted net assets. In some instances, amounts are segregated to provide for specific contingencies or other future needs, the financial requirements of which were at the moment indeterminate. Such reserves, appropriations or contingencies should not be included as liabilities, or as separate funds on an organization's balance sheet. However, the procedure that follows does provide an acceptable method for recording such provisions.

When a board wishes to indicate in the unrestricted net assets section of the balance sheet that it intends to use some portion of the net assets in a future period for a particular purpose, it may do so by designating part of the net assets. Such designations should be documented in the board minutes. For example, if the board wishes to designate $115,200 for future research purposes, the organization would report the designation within the net assets section as follows:

Unrestricted—board-designated for
special purposes $115,200

It should be noted that this designation does not result in a charge reflected in the statement of activities. Rather, all that has happened is that the board has segregated a portion of its unrestricted net assets balance to indicate its intention to spend these moneys in a certain way. During a future period, when the amounts for research are actually expended, they will be included in the expenses of the unrestricted class of net assets. The organization would then reverse its designation in the net assets section.

Usually it would not be necessary to show the details of all changes during the year in the amounts designated for specific purposes by the board on the balance sheet. Disclosure of the year-end amounts in the balance sheet would normally be sufficient. If, on the other hand, the board wished to disclose the details, it could do so in the notes to the financial statements or in a separate statement of changes in net assets.

The undesignated unrestricted net asset balance should not be reported to be in deficit position as the result of designations which exceed the total available unrestricted net assets.

The presentation of the balances of individual classes of net assets in an organization's balance sheet should conform to the nomenclature illustrated in Exhibit A and to the subclassification standards discussed in Chapter 2.

Net Assets

Financial Statements of Closely Related Organizations

This chapter covers both consolidated and combining financial statements. Consolidated (sometimes called combined) financial statements present only the total "entity," whereas combining financial statements present separately some or all of the individual entities included.

Situations exist in which voluntary health and welfare organizations are so closely related that they may reasonably be regarded as a single entity, and their financial reports should be consolidated in a single set of statements. For instance, a national organization that permits solicitation of contributions in its name by local affiliates may be expected to account for all the programs served by the contributor's dollar—nationally as well as locally—in a single set of financial statements. The same may be said of a local organization that permits an auxiliary or other volunteer group to appeal for financial support on its behalf. In such instances, only the ultimate recipient, or central organization, may be in a position to render a consolidated report of all program and supporting service uses to which contributions to any of the related organizations have been applied.

Other circumstances, apart from a central organization's permitting solicitation of support in its name by affiliated organizations, may call for consolidated financial reporting for a group of related organizations. If major program services—e.g., research, health education, direct services to individuals—or fund-raising activities of one organization are substantially financed by its affiliates, or when local fund raising is substantially financed by a national organization, consolidated financial statements for the organization and its affiliates may be indispensable for accounting to contributors to the affiliates for an important part of their contributions. If a central organization effectively has final control over the funds of one or more related organizations so as to be able to direct their use and accounting, or if the related organizations have no significant programs apart from financial support of the central organization, consolidated financial reporting for the central organization and its related organizations or other groups will usually be essential for complete and meaningful financial disclosure.

Standards for Consolidated Financial Statements

Consolidated financial statements may provide better information than separate statements. However, the state of the art in this area is in flux.

The AICPA Statement of Position No. 94-3, Reporting of Related Entities by Not-for-Profit Organizations (included in the audit and accounting guide Not-for-Profit Organizations) indicates that the question depends on the nature of the relationship between the organizations, specifically the extent to which one organization both controls and has an economic interest in the other organization.

The FASB is also studying the issue of what constitutes the reporting entity, and final accounting standards must await the conclusion of that effort.

Voluntary health and welfare organizations should adopt consolidated reporting when the criteria of SOP 94-3 are met, which is when it is helpful in achieving comprehensive accounting to the public for activities of units effectively controlled—e.g., for a local organization and supporting auxiliaries, for a state organization and its local chapters.

SOP 94-3 states that: "In the case of (a) . . . control through a majority voting interest in the board of the other entity and (b) an economic interest in other such organizations, consolidation is required. . . ." [There are certain exceptions, and certain other criteria applicable to less common circumstances, for which the original SOP should be consulted.]

The definitions of control and economic interest are:

Control. The direct or indirect ability to determine the direction of management and policies through ownership, contract or otherwise.

Economic interest. An interest in another entity that exists if (a) the other entity holds or utilizes significant resources that must be used for the unrestricted or restricted purposes of the not-for-profit organization, either directly or indirectly by producing income or providing services, or (b) the reporting organization is responsible for the liabilities of the other entity. The following are examples of economic interests:

- Other entities solicit funds in the name of and with the expressed or implied approval of the reporting organization, and substantially all of the funds solicited are intended by the contributor or are otherwise required to be transferred to the reporting organization, or used at its discretion or direction.

- A reporting organization transfers significant resources to another entity whose resources are held for the benefit of the reporting organization.

- A reporting organization assigns certain significant functions to another entity.

- A reporting organization provides or is committed to provide funds for another entity, or guarantees significant debt of another entity.

If control exists through factors other than a majority voting interest, and if there is an economic interest, then consolidation is permitted but not required; if, in this case, the affiliate is not consolidated, certain additional disclosures are required.

If there is control or an economic interest, but not both, then consolidation is not permitted, but certain disclosures are required.

The above rules are presented in the flowchart at the end of this chapter.

In cases where a not-for-profit entity owns a voting economic interest in a for-profit entity, the normal rules applicable to for-profit owners should be followed. These are discussed in SOP 94-3 and documents referred to therein.

For annual reporting pursuant to these standards, a voluntary health and welfare organization should present a single set of consolidated (or combining, if it wishes) financial statements for itself, and for all of its affiliated organizations or groups to which the foregoing criteria apply. They should be understood as applicable both to local and to national organizations, and to unincorporated auxiliaries, guilds, circles, committees and other organized groups associated with a health or welfare organization, as well as to incorporated organizations.

Legally unrestricted net assets of organizations related to the reporting organization may be effectively restricted with respect to the reporting organization. In consolidated financial statements that include both the related organization and the reporting organization, it may be appropriate to present all net assets of the related organization, both unrestricted and temporarily restricted, as temporarily restricted net assets.

A national or international organization may have state or local chapters with varying degrees of autonomy. Affiliated organizations may be separate corporate entities or unincorporated boards, committees, or chapters. A national or "parent" organization with loosely affiliated local organizations whose resources are principally derived and expended locally, normally would not consolidate the local organizations' financial statements with its own. Some of the characteristics of a loose affiliation are:

1. Locally determined program activities

2. Financial independence of the local organization

3. Control of its assets by the local organization

See section below "Consolidated Financial Statements Control Factors."

Disclosure of Basis of Financial Statement Consolidation

The basis for consolidating financial statements should be disclosed in the notes to the financial statements, including the interrelationship of the organizations, and a description of the entities.

If affiliated organizations are not consolidated because they do not meet the above combining criteria, the existence of the affiliates and their relationships to the reporting organizations should be disclosed.

Financial reporting that purports to present the consolidated financial statements of a group of related organizations may fairly be assumed, in the absence of qualifying explanations, to include all affiliates of the reporting organization. When such statements omit any organizations closely related to the reporting organization, the basis for the omission should be clearly described in the headings of the statements or in a note accompanying them.

In consolidating financial statements of related organizations, the final step is the addition of all major report classifications of the related organizations to obtain totals for the entire group. If the total in each resulting accounting classification is to conform to the respective definition in this report, the individual accounts of the organizations being consolidated must be maintained in conformity with the definitions in Standards. In addition, central and affiliated organizations must maintain reciprocal accounts for transactions with each other—e.g., collected through local

Conforming Subordinate Unit Accounting to Consolidated Financial Reporting

member units and paid to a national organization on the books of a national organization—campaign proceeds on the books of a local. This will permit elimination of intragroup transactions that would otherwise inflate contributions, or other account totals, reported for the group as a single entity (in effect, preventing double reporting of contributions or other items).

Consolidated Financial Statements Control Factors

This section is presented to provide additional guidance in helping organizations decide whether or not it is appropriate to issue consolidated financial statements for the reporting entity and its affiliates. The following compares factors that indicate control vs. factors that suggest lack of control, in an outline form.

FACTORS WHICH MAY INDICATE THAT AN AFFILIATED NOT-FOR-PROFIT ORGANIZATION (A) IS CONTROLLED BY THE REPORTING ORGANIZATION (R)

- Following is a list of factors which may be helpful to not-for-profit organizations, in determining whether an affiliated not-for-profit organization is controlled as contemplated by AICPA SOP 94-3 (par. 8 and Glossary);

- Many of these factors are not determinative by themselves, but must be considered in conjunction with other factors.

Factors Whose Presence Indicate Control	Factors Whose Presence Indicate Absence of Control
Governance:	
1. A's board has considerable overlap in membership with R; common officers.	1. There is little or no overlap.
2. A's board members and/or officers are appointed by R, or are subject to approval of R's board, officers, or members.	2. A's board is self perpetuating without input from R.
3. Major decisions of A's board, officers or staff are subject to review, approval or ratification by R.	3. A's decisions are made autonomously; or even if in theory subject to such control, R has in fact never or rarely exercised control and does not intend to do so.
Financial:	
4. A's budget is subject to review or approval by R.	4. A's budget is not subject to R's approval.
5. Some or all of A's disbursements are subject to approval or countersignature by R.	5. Checks may be issued without R's approval.
6. A's excess of revenue over expenses or net assets, or portions thereof, are subject to being transferred to R at R's request, or are automatically transferred.	6. Although some of A's financial resources may be transferred to R, this is done only at the discretion of A's board.
7. A's activities are largely financed by grants, loans or transfers from R, or from other sources determined by R's board.	7. A's activities are financed from sources determined by A's board.
8. A's by-laws indicate that its resources are intended to be used for activities similar to those of R.	8. A's by-laws limit uses of resources to purposes which do not include R's activities.

Public perception of the relationship:

9. A is clearly described as controlled by, for the benefit of, or an affiliate of R in some of the following:
   - articles/charter/by-laws
   - operating/affiliation agreement
   - fund-raising/membership brochure
   - annual report
   - grant proposals
   - application for tax-exempt status.

9. A is described as independent of R, or no formal relationship is indicated.

10. A's fund-raising appeals give donors the impression that gifts will be used to further R's programs.

10. Appeals give the impression that resources will be used by A.

Operating:

11. A shares with R many of the following operating functions:
    - personnel/payroll/office space
    - purchasing/accounting/treasury
    - professional services
    - fund-raising

11. Few operating functions are shared; or reimbursement of costs is on a strictly arms-length basis with formal contracts.

12. Decisions about A's program or other activities are made by R or are subject to R's review or approval.

12. A's decisions are made autonomously.

13. A's activities are almost exclusively for the benefit of R's members.

13. Activities benefit persons unaffiliated with R.

Other:

14. A is exempt under Internal Revenue Code Section 501(c)(3) and R is exempt under some other subsection of 501(c), and A's main purpose for existence appears to be to solicit tax deductible contributions to further R's interests.

14. A's purposes include significant activities apart from those of R.

15. A meets the public support test under IRC Section 509(a) by virtue of it being a supporting organization to R. 509(a)(3)

15. Factor not present.

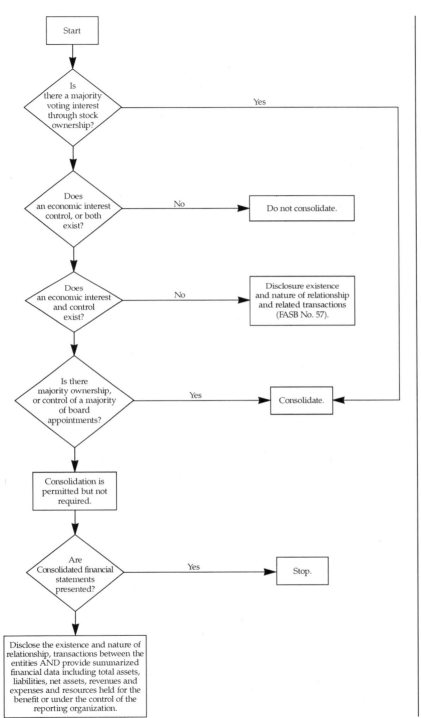

Start

Is there a majority voting interest through stock ownership? — Yes →

Does an economic interest control, or both exist? — No → Do not consolidate.

Does an economic interest and control exist? — No → Disclosure existence and nature of relationship and related transactions (FASB No. 57).

Is there majority ownership, or control of a majority of board appointments? — Yes → Consolidate.

Consolidation is permitted but not required.

Are Consolidated financial statements presented? — Yes → Stop.

Disclose the existence and nature of relationship, transactions between the entities AND provide summarized financial data including total assets, liabilities, net assets, revenues and expenses and resources held for the benefit or under the control of the reporting organization.

Illustrative Financial Statements

The Standards provides uniform accounting and financial reporting procedures sufficiently detailed and extensive to meet the reporting needs, at one extreme, of small local organizations and, at the other, of very large national organizations. The preceding chapters have necessarily attempted to treat the wide variations in sources of support and revenue, and types of net assets and balance sheet accounts, of the different voluntary health and welfare organizations. Illustrative forms of financial statements for public reporting reflecting these accounting standards are presented in the following pages. They represent a single set of financial statements of a medium-sized, affiliated voluntary organization. In the preparation of combined financial statements for all affiliated entities of an organization, whether at the state or national level, transactions between the entities would be eliminated. Accordingly, the captions in Exhibits B and C regarding public support from local member units, payments to national organizations, etc., would not appear in consolidated financial statements.

The revenue section of Exhibit B illustrates more accounts than an organization is likely to need. All organizations—of whatever size, whether at the local, state or national level, and whether affiliated or fully independent—may present statements simplified to meet their own requirements by the omission of those items not applicable to their operations. On the other hand, the accounts in earned revenue, expenses and other classifications may prove inadequate for some large and complex organizations. As previously suggested, organizations in designing their financial statements may choose to supplement or expand categories shown in the illustrated statements to suit their needs. At the same time, they should conform this supplementation and expansion with the classifications and categories of the illustrated statements.

Regardless of its size or the simplicity of its financial structure, every organization seeking to conform its annual financial reports to the Standards should include, in one report, at least the following four forms of statements and accompanying notes:

- Balance Sheet

- Statement of Activities

- Statement of Functional Expenses

- Statement of Cash Flows

Illustrative Financial Statements

The illustrated forms of Exhibits A and B are a multicolumn presentation. A one column presentation is also acceptable, as long as total unrestricted, temporarily restricted and permanently restricted net assets are reported.

Expenses appearing on Exhibit B, in particular program services and supporting services, are derived from Exhibit C.

Organizations should include notes to their financial statements that provide any additional information needed for fair presentation, such as significant accounting policies, mortgage agreements, pension plans, contingent liabilities, etc. In every case, the standard of public financial reporting to follow is to report all significant facts necessary to make an organization's financial statements fully informative and not misleading. It is thus recommended (and in many states required) that, to fulfill its obligation to the contributing public, the accounts of a voluntary health or welfare organization be examined annually, in accordance with generally accepted accounting principles by independent auditors.

Voluntary organizations are encouraged to include in their published audited financial statements separate columns showing comparative data for the preceding year. Their repetition in an organization's current statements may be expected to improve a reader's understanding of the report and his or her grasp of its significance. When using a columnar format, presentation of only the prior year total column will often be sufficient for this purpose.

It should be noted that the amounts shown in the accompanying statements have been included for illustrative purposes only. No attempt has been made to conform them to relationships exhibited by financial data of any group of voluntary organizations nor to suggest particular relationships. Modifications to the illustrated financial statements should be made to fit the facts and circumstances of each specific organization.

NOTE: For illustrated financial statements of United Ways and Federated Fund-raising Organizations, see Appendix 2.

Balance Sheet

VOLUNTARY HEALTH AND WELFARE AFFILIATE

Balance Sheet
December 31, 19x2 with Comparative Totals for 19x1

Assets	Unrestricted	Restricted	Total 19x2	Total 19x1
Cash and cash equivalents (Note 3)	$ 110,400	$ 11,000	$ 121,400	$ 127,000
Investments, at—market value (Note 5)	421,500	160,000	581,500	552,400
Receivables:				
Program service fees, less allowance				
of $200 (19x1—$100)	600		600	800
Pledges, at fair value, less allowance of				
of $11,200 (19x1—$9,711) (Notes 4 & 6)	58,900		58,900	46,000
Grants	4,800	1,000	5,800	4,600
From affiliated organizations	1,000		1,000	1,000
Inventory, at lower of cost or market	7,000		7,000	6,100
Prepaid expenses and deferred charges	13,800		13,800	9,600
Land, buildings and equipment, at cost,				
less accumulated depreciation (Note 7)	173,800		173,800	167,500
Other Assets	1,000		1,000	1,000
Interfund receivable (payable)	2,000	(2,000)	—	
Total assets	$ 794,800	$ 170,000	$ 964,800	$ 916,000
LIABILITIES AND NET ASSETS				
Accounts Payable and accrued expenses	$ 39,300		$ 39,300	$ 46,000
Research grants (Note 6)	41,600		41,600	45,600
Refundable advances	18,000		18,000	16,000
Mortgage payable, 6%, due 19xx (Note 14)	3,200		3,200	3,600
Amounts payable under capital leases				
(Note 12)	10,200		10,200	
Total liabilities	112,300	—	112,300	111,200
Net Assets:				
Unrestricted:				
Fund A	241,500		$ 241,500	246,100
Fund B	279,600		279,600	239,000
Fund C	161,400		161,400	154,700
Temporarily restricted (Note 10)		50,000	50,000	55,000
Permanently restricted (Note 10)		120,000	120,000	110,000
Total net assets	682,500	170,000	852,500	804,800
Total liabilities and net assets	$ 794,800	$ 170,000	$ 964,800	$ 916,000

The accompanying notes are an integral part of these financial statements

Statement of Activities

EXHIBIT B

VOLUNTARY HEALTH AND WELFARE SERVICE AFFILIATE

Statement of Activities
For the year ended December 31, 19x2 with Comparative Totals for 19x1

	Unrestricted				Restricted		Total	
	Fund A	Fund B	Fund C	Fund D	Temporarily	Permanently	19x2	19x1
Revenue:								
Public support—								
Received directly—								
Contributions, at fair value (Note 2)	$625,700	$ 27,800	$ 7,200	$660,700	$ 3,000	$10,000	$673,700	$700,400
Special events	28,400			28,400			28,400	25,500
Less: Direct benefit costs	(18,000)			(18,000)			(18,000)	(16,300)
Legacies and bequests	9,600			9,600			9,600	12,000
Contributed services, at fair value (Note 8)	8,000			8,000			8,000	7,000
Received indirectly from—								
Local member units	4,000			4,000			4,000	7,900
Federated fund-raising organizations	23,500			23,500			23,500	22,000
Total public support	681,200	27,800	7,200	716,200	3,000	10,000	729,200	758,500
Revenue and grants from governmental agencies					300		300	300
Other revenues:								
Membership dues-individuals	500			500			500	400
Assessments and dues-local member units	1,100			1,100			1,100	700
Program service fees	2,300			2,300			2,300	800
Sales of materials and services	400			400			400	300
Investment income	16,200			16,200	15,000		31,200	26,000
Other	2,800			2,800			2,800	3,600
Gains (losses) on investments	200			200	300		500	27,500
Total other revenue	23,500	—	—	23,500	15,300	—	38,800	59,300
Net Assets released from restrictions (Note 11):								
Satisfaction of program restrictions		10,800		10,800	(10,800)			
Expiration of time restrictions		12,800		12,800	(12,800)			
Total revenue	704,700	51,400	7,200	763,300	(5,000)	10,000	768,300	818,100
Expenses:								
Program services—								
Program A	141,200		200	141,400			141,400	136,500
Program B	53,900		500	54,400			54,400	48,500
Program C	61,200		600	61,800			61,800	51,600
Program D	244,100	10,800	2,900	257,800			257,800	273,600
Total program services	500,400	10,800	4,200	515,400			515,400	510,200
Supporting services—								
Management and General	56,800		600	57,400			57,400	63,800
Fund-raising	65,000		400	65,400			65,400	54,600
Total supporting services	121,800	—	1,000	122,800			122,800	118,400
Payments to national organization (Note 13)	82,400			82,400			82,400	85,400
Total expenses	704,600	10,800	5,200	720,600			720,600	714,000
Excess (deficiency) of revenue over expenses	100	40,600	2,000	42,700	(5,000)	10,000	47,700	104,100
Transfers	(4,700)		4,700	—				
Total changes in net assets	(4,600)	40,600	6,700	42,700	(5,000)	10,000	47,700	104,100
Net assets, beginning of year	246,100	239,000	154,700	639,800	55,000	110,000	804,800	700,700
Net assets, end of year	$ 241,500	$ 279,600	$161,400	$ 682,500	$50,000	$120,000	$852,500	$804,800

The accompanying notes are an integral part of these financial statements

147

Statement of Functional Expenses

EXHIBIT C

VOLUNTARY HEALTH AND WELFARE SERVICE AFFILIATE

Statement of Functional Expenses
For the year ended December 31, 19x2 with Comparative Totals for 19x1

	Program Services					Supporting Services			Total Expenses	
	Program A	Program B	Program C	Program D	Total	Management & General	Fund-raising	Total	19x2	19x1
Salaries	$ 4,500	$29,100	$ 25,100	$ 116,900	$ 175,600	$ 33,100	$ 36,800	$69,900	$245,500	$233,300
Employee Benefits	400	1,400	1,400	6,400	9,600	2,200	1,500	3,700	13,300	12,500
Payroll taxes, etc.	400	2,600	2,300	12,400	17,700	3,000	3,100	6,100	23,800	21,500
Total salaries and related expenses	5,300	33,100	28,800	135,700	202,900	38,300	41,400	79,700	282,600	267,300
Professional fees		1,000	300	1,200	2,500	2,600	800	3,400	5,900	5,300
Supplies	600	1,300	1,300	1,300	4,500	1,800	1,700	3,500	8,000	7,100
Telecommunications services	200	300	1,000	1,100	2,600	1,500	2,300	3,800	6,400	6,800
Postage and shipping	200	1,700	1,300	8,900	12,100	1,000	9,000	10,000	22,100	8,000
Occupancy	250	1,300	1,100	1,250	3,900	1,500	1,350	2,850	6,750	6,300
Interest				100	100	800		800	900	200
Rental and maintenance of equipment	250	1,300	1,100	1,250	3,900	1,500	1,350	2,850	6,750	6,300
Printing and publications		2,400	400	6,400	9,200	300	1,600	1,900	11,100	5,800
Travel and transportation	300	2,200	2,000	2,200	6,700	2,300	3,000	5,300	12,000	11,300
Conferences, conventions & meetings	800	1,900	7,100	2,000	11,800	4,500	400	4,900	16,700	15,600
Specific assistance to individuals		6,500	4,300		10,800			—	10,800	18,400
Membership dues		500			500			—	500	500
Payments to National Organizations—Research				10,000	10,000			—	10,000	10,000
Awards and grants To national organizations				83,000	83,000			—	83,000	104,200
To individuals & other organizations	133,200		11,900		145,100			—	145,100	144,300
Insurance	50	200	100	100	450	600	50	650	1,100	1,000
Other Expenses	50	200	500	400	1,150	100	2,050	2,150	3,300	5,600
Depreciation of buildings & equipment	200	500	600	2,900	4,200	600	400	1,000	5,200	4,600
Total functional expenses	$141,400	$54,400	$61,800	$257,800	$515,400	$57,400	$65,400	$122,800	$638,200	$628,600
Unallocated payments to affiliates									82,400	85,400
Total expenses									720,600	714,000
Direct benefit costs									18,000	16,300
Total expenses and direct benefit costs									$738,600	$730,300

The accompanying notes are an integral part of these financial statements

Statement of Cash Flows
Indirect Method

VOLUNTARY HEALTH AND WELFARE SERVICE AFFILIATE

Statement of Cash Flows
For the year ended December 31, 19x2 with Comparative Totals for 19x1

			Total	
	Unrestricted	Restricted	19x2	19x1
Cash flows from operating activities:				
Change in net assets	$ 42,700	$ 5,000	$ 47,700	$ 104,100
Adjustments to reconcile change in net assets to				
net cash provided (used by operating activities):				
Depreciation and amortization	5,200		5,200	4,600
Net (gains) losses on sales of securities	(1,000)	500	(500)	(27,500)
Contributions restricted for long-term investment		(10,000)	(10,000)	(40,000)
Changes in assets and liabilities:				
(Increase)/decrease in receivables	(12,900)	(1,000)	(13,900)	7,000
(Increase)/decrease in inventory	(900)		(900)	1,500
(Increase)/decrease in prepaid expenses and				
deferred expenses	(4,200)		(4,200)	(1,000)
(Increase)/decrease in other assets	—			(1,000)
Increase/(decrease) in accounts payable and				
accrued expenses	(6,700)		(6,700)	5,000
Increase/(decrease) in research grants	(4,000)		(4,000)	3,200
Increase/(decrease) in refundable advance	2,000		2,000	(2,500)
Net cash provided (used) by operating activities	20,200	(5,500)	14,700	53,400
Cash flows from investing activities:				
Purchase of equipment	(11,500)		(11,500)	(7,000)
Proceeds from sale of equipment			—	1,000
Proceeds from sale of investments	1,000		1,000	50,000
Purchase of investments	(19,600)	(10,000)	(29,600)	(86,000)
Net cash used by investing activities	(30,100)	(10,000)	(40,100)	(42,000)
Cash flows from financing activities:				
Proceeds from contributions restricted for:				
Investment in endowment		10,000	10,000	40,000
Investment in land, building & equipment			—	1,000
Other financing activities			—	
Payments on mortgage payable	(400)		(400)	(400)
Proceeds from capital lease obligation	10,200		10,200	
Net cash provided by financing activities	9,800	10,000	19,800	40,600
Net increase (decrease) in cash & cash equivalents	(100)	(5,500)	(5,600)	52,000
Cash & cash equivalents, beginning of year	110,500	16,500	127,000	75,000
Cash & cash equivalents, end of year	$ 110,400	$ 11,000	$ 121,400	$ 127,000
Supplemental disclosure of cash flow information—				
cash paid during the year for interest	$ 900		$ 900	$ 200

The accompanying notes are an integral part of these financial statements

151

Statement of Cash Flows
Direct Method

VOLUNTARY HEALTH AND WELFARE SERVICE AFFILIATE

Statement of Cash Flows
For the year ended December 31, 19x2 with Comparative Totals for 19x1

	Unrestricted	Restricted	Total 19x2	19x1
Cash flows from operating activities:				
Cash received from service recipients	$ 2,300		$ 2,300	$ 800
Cash received from contributors	667,300		667,300	720,000
Cash collected on pledges receivable	46,000		46,000	54,000
Cash received from sales of materials & services	1,200		1,200	1,000
Interest & dividends received	16,200	15,000	31,200	26,000
Miscellaneous receipts	20,000		20,000	17,500
Interest paid	(900)		(900)	(200)
Cash paid to employees & suppliers	(500,000)		(500,000)	(510,000)
Grants paid	(228,100)		(228,100)	(248,500)
Miscellaneous payments	(3,800)	(20,500)	(24,300)	(7,200)
Net cash provided (used) by operation activities	20,200	(5,500)	14,700	53,400
Cash flows from investing activities:				
Purchase of equipment	(11,500)		(11,500)	(7,000)
Proceeds from sale of equipment	—		—	1,000
Proceeds from sale of investments	1,000		1,000	50,000
Purchase of investments	(19,600)	(10,000)	(29,600)	(86,000)
Net cash used by investing activities	(30,100)	(10,000)	(40,100)	(42,000)
Cash flows from financing activities:				
Proceeds from contributions restricted for:				
Investment in endowment		10,000	10,000	40,000
Investment in land, building & equipment			—	1,000
Other financing activities:				
Payments on mortgage payable	(400)		(400)	(400)
Proceeds from capital lease obligation	10,200		10,200	
Net cash provided by financing activities	9,800	10,000	19,800	40,600
Net increase (decrease) in cash & cash equivalents	(100)	(5,500)	(5,600)	52,000
Cash & cash equivalents, beginning of year	110,500	16,500	127,000	75,000
Cash & cash equivalents, end of year	$ 110,400	$ 11,000	$ 121,400	$ 127,000
Reconciliation of change in net assets to net cash provided (used) by operating activities				
Change in net assets	$ 42,700	$ 5,000	$ 47,700	$ 104,100
Adjustment to reconcile change in net assets to net cash provided (used) by operating activities:				
Depreciation & amortization	5,200		5,200	4,600
Net (gains)/losses on sales of securities	(1,000)	500	(500)	(27,500)
(Increase)/decrease in receivable	(12,900)	(1,000)	(13,900)	7,000
(Increase)/decrease in inventory	(900)		(900)	1,500
(Increase)/decrease in prepaid expenses & deferred expenses	(4,200)		(4,200)	(1,000)
(Increase)/decrease in other assets			—	(1,000)
(Increase)/decrease in accounts payable & accrued expenses	(6,700)		(6,700)	5,000
(Increase)/decrease in research grants	(4,000)		(4,000)	3,200
(Increase)/decrease in refundable advance	2,000		2,000	(2,500)
Contributions restricted for long-term investment		(10,000)	(10,000)	(40,000)
Net cash provided (used) by operating activities	$ 20,200	$ (5,500)	$ 14,700	$ 53,400

The accompanying notes are an integral part of these financial statements

Voluntary Health and Welfare Service Affiliate Notes to Financial Statements December 31, 19X2

CHAPTER

NOTES

1. Organization (the "Service"), is a local unit of the National Voluntary Health and Welfare Service. Its principal programs include: Research—financial support provided to academic institutions and scientists seeking knowledge of the causes, cures and prevention of _____ disease; Public Health Education—programs designed to promote effective health practices; Professional Health Education—programs designed to improve the knowledge and skills of the medical and allied professions in the prevention, detection and diagnosis and treatment of patients; and Community Health Services—services provided for conduct of rehabilitation and other patient programs, planning and improving community health practices, and supporting clinics and other health facilities. The Service also cooperates and assists in the local fund-raising activities of the national organization.

The financial statements do not include assets, liabilities, revenues and expenses of the Voluntary Health and Welfare Service Foundation, a separate organization not controlled by the Service, whose purpose is to raise money to provide additional assistance directly to clients of the Service's facilities.

The Service is exempt from income tax under Section 501(c)(3) of the U.S. Internal Revenue Code and comparable State law, and contributions to it are tax deductible within the limitations prescribed by the Code. The Service has been classified as a publicly-supported organization which is not a private foundation under Section 509(a) of the Code.

(If the organization chooses to present only summarized information for the prior period, the following disclosure is required: The financial statements include certain prior-year summarized comparative information in total but not by net

asset class. Such information does not include sufficient detail to constitute a presentation in accordance with generally accepted accounting principles. Accordingly, such information should be read in conjunction with the financial statements for the year ended December 31, 19X1, from which the summarized information was derived.)

2. *Significant Accounting Policies*—The financial statements report amounts separately by class of net assets as follows:

- Unrestricted amounts are those currently available for use under the direction of the board, those designated by the board for specific uses, and resources invested in fixed assets.

- Temporarily restricted amounts are those restricted by donors for specific purposes or for the acquisition of fixed assets, or for use in specific future periods or after the occurrence of a specified event.

- Permanently restricted amounts are those restricted by donors in perpetuity as endowments.

All contributions are considered available for unrestricted use, unless specifically restricted by the donor or received in the form of pledges. Amounts received that are designated for future periods, are in the form of pledges, or are restricted by the donor for specific purposes, are reported as temporarily restricted or permanently restricted support that increases those net asset classes. However, if a restriction on a contribution or on investment income is fulfilled in the same time period in which the related income is received, the Service reports the income as unrestricted. *[Note: Organizations have a choice of policy here. See third sentence of paragraph 14 of SFAS 116. The policies followed with respect to contributions and investment income must be the same.]* When a donor restriction expires, that is, when a stipulated time restriction ends or purpose restriction is accomplished, temporarily restricted net assets are reclassified to unrestricted net assets, and reported in the statement of activities as net assets released from restrictions.

Unconditional promises to give that are expected to be collected within one year are recorded at their net realizable value. Unconditional promises to give that are expected to be collected in future years are recorded at the present value of the amounts expected to be collected. Conditional promises to give are not included as support until such time as the conditions are substantially met. Bequests are recorded as income at the time the Service has an established right to the bequest and the proceeds are measurable.

Allocation of Expenses—The costs of providing the various program services and supporting activities have been summarized on a functional basis in the statement of activities. Accordingly, certain costs have been allocated among the various functions. In 19X2, the Service incurred joint costs of $9,600 for informational materials and activities that included fund-raising appeals. Of those costs, $6,100 was allocated to fund-raising expense, $400 was allocated to Program B expense, $2,400 was allocated to Program D expense and $700 was allocated to management and general expense.

Use of Estimates—The preparation of financial statements in accordance with generally accepted accounting principles requires management to make estimates and assumptions that affect the reported amounts of assets and liabilities at the date of the financial statements and the reported amounts of revenues and expenses during the reporting period. Actual results could differ from those estimates.

Additional accounting policies are included in other footnotes. *[Organizations may wish to present all accounting policies in this footnote.]*

3. *Statement of Cash Flows*—For purposes of reporting cash flows, cash includes demand deposits with banks or financial institutions, on-hand currency, and other kinds of accounts that have the general characteristics of demand deposits. Cash equivalents include short-term investments with original maturities of three months or less.

4. *Estimated Fair Values*—For purposes of disclosing fair values, financial instruments included cash and cash equivalents, investments, receivables and accounts, research grants and mortgages payable. Cash and cash equivalents, receivables (other than pledges) and accounts and research grants payable are deemed to be stated at their fair values. Investments in equity securities with readily determinable fair values, and all debt securities, are stated at fair values, based upon quoted market prices. Pledges receivable are stated at their fair values, based upon the timing of expected future cash flows. Based upon current borrowing rates, the fair value of mortgages payable is $1,700 (19X1—$2,000).

5. *Investments*—Investments in marketable equity securities, bonds and investment account cash balances are reported at fair value. Historical costs, quoted market values and aggregate unrealized gains (losses) are summarized as follows:

	Quoted Market Value	Historical Cost	Unrealized Gain/(Loss)
Unrestricted Fund:			
Cash	$120,000	$120,000	$ 0
Corporate Bonds	220,000	210,500	9,500
Common Stocks	81,500	79,200	2,300
	$421,500	$409,700	$11,800
Research Restricted Fund:			
Cash	$ 50,000	$ 50,000	$ 0
Corporate Bonds	80,000	75,500	4,500
Common Stocks	30,000	27,800	2,200
	$160,000	$153,300	$ 6,700

6. *Pledges, Awards, and Grants*—Unconditional promises expected to be collected within one year are presented at their net realizable value. Those expected in more than one year are reported at the present value of their estimated future cash flows using a risk-free interest rate at the date of the pledge to determine the discounts. Amortization of the

discounts is included in contribution revenue. Pledges receivable are as follows:

Unconditional promises receivable (pledges) before unamortized discount and allowance for uncollectibles	$76,700
Less unamortized discount	6,600
	70,100
Less allowance for uncollectibles	11,200
Net pledges receivable	$58,900
Amounts due in:	
Less than one year	$31,500
One to five years	36,700
More than five years	8,500
	$76,700

Discount rates ranged from 5.5% to 6.5% for the pledges due in more than one year.

In 19X2 the Service received a promise to contribute $10,000 if a similar amount is raised from other sources by the end of 19X3. Revenue related to this pledge will be recorded only when the matching amount is raised.

In addition, the Service has received from a manufacturer of medical supplies an indication of an intention to give a significant amount of such supplies. No amount has been recorded related to this intention.

The Service's awards and grants to others are recorded as liabilities and expenses when voted by its governing board. These are payable as follows:

Less than one year	$23,000
One to five years	5,600
More than five years	17,100
Less discount to present value	(4,100)
Total	$41,600

7. *Land, Buildings, Equipment and Depreciation*—The Service follows the practice of capitalizing all expenditures for land, buildings and equipment in excess of $500; the fair value of donated fixed assets is similarly capitalized. Depreciation of buildings and equipment is provided on a straight-line basis over the estimated useful lives of the assets (2 percent per year for buildings, 10 percent for medical research equipment and office furniture and equipment, and 33 percent for the automobile). At December 31, 19X2 such assets were:

	19X2
Land	$ 35,600
Buildings	100,000
Medical research equipment	33,600
Office furniture and equipment	24,600
Automobile	8,000
Total	201,800
Less accumulated depreciation	28,000
	$173,800

8. *Donated Materials and Services*—Donated materials and equipment are reflected as contributions in the accompanying statements at their estimated values at date of receipt. If donors stipulate how long the assets must be used, the contributions are recorded as restricted support. In the absence of such stipulations, contributions of materials and equipment are recorded as unrestricted support.

Donated services include approximately 1,000 hours of skilled services provided by volunteers in the public health education and community health services programs. The fair value (at $8 per hour) of donated services meeting the criteria of SFAS 116 is recorded as contributions and salary expense in the period rendered.

In addition, a substantial number of other volunteers have donated over 5,000 hours of their time in the organization's program services and its fund-raising campaigns.

Standards of Accounting and Financial Reporting

9. *Pension Plan—(Statement of Financial Accounting Standards No. 132, Employers' Disclosures about Pensions and Other Postretirement Benefits, permits some organizations to provide less extensive disclosure in this Note.)* The Service has a defined benefit pension plan covering substantially all of its employees. The benefits are based on years of service and the employee's compensation during the last five years of employment. The funding policy is to fund pension cost accrued. Contributions are intended to provide not only for benefits attributed to service to date, but also for those expected to be earned in the future.

The following table sets forth the plan's funded status and amounts recognized in the balance sheet at December 31, 19X2:

Actuarial present value of benefit obligations:

Accumulated benefit obligation, including vested benefits of $2,870	$(3,350)
Projected benefit obligation for services rendered to date	$(5,000)
Plan assets at fair value, primarily listed stocks and U.S. bonds	4,750
Projected benefit obligation in excess of plan assets	(250)
Unrecognized net gain from past experience different from that assumed and effects of changes in assumptions	(530)
Prior service cost not yet recognized in net periodic pension cost	190
Unrecognized net obligation at January 1, 1986, being recognized over 15 years	770
Prepaid pension cost included in deferred charges	$ 180

Net pension cost included the following components:

	19X2
Service cost (benefits earned during the period)	$260
Interest cost on projected benefit obligation	390
Actual return on plan assets	(450)
Net amortization and deferral	100
Net periodic pension cost	$300

The weighted-average discount rate and rate of increase in future compensation levels used in determining the actuarial present value of the projected benefit obligation were 7 percent and 5 percent, respectively, in both years. The expected long-term rate of return on assets was 8 percent in 19X2.

The Service has a defined contribution retirement plan covering substantially all of its employees. The Service matches each employee's contribution to the plan, with each employee's contribution being limited to a percentage of salary. Contributions by the Service are fully vested to the employees on the contribution date. The retirement plan contribution included in expenses was $300 in 19X2.

Other Post-Retirement Benefits—The Service provides certain health care and life insurance benefits for retired employees. Substantially all of the employees may become eligible for this benefit if they reach normal retirement age while still working for the Service. Those benefits and similar benefits for active employees are provided through insurance companies whose premiums are based on the benefits paid during the year. The Service recognized the cost of providing those benefits by expensing the annual insurance premiums, which were $3,044 in 19X2. Of this amount, $960 was applicable to retirees.

10. *Restricted Net Assets*—Temporarily restricted net assets are available for the following purposes or periods:

Program A Activities	$20,000
Program B Activities	10,000
Program D Activities	15,000
For periods after December 31, 19X2	5,000
	$50,000

Permanently restricted net assets are restricted to investment in perpetuity, the income from which is expendable to support:

Program A Activities	$ 35,000
Program C Activities	50,000
Program D Activities	32,000
Any activities of the organization	3,000
	$120,000

11. *Net Assets Released From Restrictions*—Net assets were released from donor restrictions by incurring expenses satisfying the restricted purposes or by occurrence of events specified by donors.

Purpose restrictions accomplished:

Program A expenses	$ 4,000
Program D expenses	6,800
	$10,800
Time restriction expired:	
Passage of specified time	8,000
Death of annuity beneficiary	4,800
	12,800
Total restrictions released	$23,600

12. *Lease Commitments*—The Service rents certain office equipment under a capital lease, expiring in 19X9. Payments under this lease are as follows:

19X3–19X8 at $2,000 per year	$12,000
19X9	700
Total lease payments	$12,700
Less amount representing interest	2,500
Present value of lease payments	$10,200

The following is a schedule, by years, of the approximate future minimum rental payments required under operating leases that have initial or remaining noncancelable lease terms in excess of one year as of December 31, 19X2:

Fiscal Year:

19X3	$3,000
19X4	3,000
19X5	3,000
19X6	2,000
19X7	3,000
later, to 2002	30,000

Rental expense aggregated approximately $5,000 in 19X2.

13. *Sharing of Public Support*—In accordance with the affiliation agreement with the national organization, 12 percent of most unrestricted support from the public is remitted to the national organization for its use as determined by its board of directors. Additional grants are made as determined by the Service's board of directors; these amounts being shown as awards and grants in the Statement of Functional Expenses.

14. *Mortgage*—The mortgage is secured by the Service's land and buildings. It is payable in monthly installments to the State Bank.

15. *Related parties*—As described in Note 1, an unconsolidated affiliated organization conducts certain activities related to the Service's programs. This affiliate rented office space from the Service for which it paid rent of $xxx, which is considered to be a fair rental for the space. At December 31, 19X2, the affiliate owed the Service $xxx representing one month's rent. Two members of the board of the Service also sit on the board of this affiliate.

16. *Contingency*—As of December 31, 19X2, a lawsuit was pending related to an accident on the Service's premises. As of March 19X3, the case was still in process of discovery. Based on a review of the facts of the case, management believes that the likelihood of a material loss from this litigation is remote.

Methods of Expense Allocation

The functional expense accounting standards described in Chapter 5 require voluntary health and welfare organizations to maintain records that reflect the classification of expenses both as to object and function. This Appendix examines the kind of expense accounting called for in Chapter 5 to promote uniformity in application and to minimize additional work in complying with the Standards.

The appendix introduces concepts and techniques of Activity Based Management (ABM) and Activity Based Costing (ABC) that may be used as a key driver for functionally allocating expenses to program and supporting services categories. These techniques can result in providing better quality information (management oriented and function oriented) while reducing the complexities which the non-profit organization must overcome in meeting the numerous and diverse reporting requirements associated with the operations of an non-profit organization.

Voluntary health and welfare organizations vary greatly in size, complexity of their activities and staff resources. Thousands of small organizations are administered entirely by volunteers. Each organization must adapt its accounting operation to its own activities, organization and staff resources. The following paragraphs suggest a practical approach to functional accounting that is adequate for public financial reporting.

In developing its functional accounting procedures, organizations should consult with their independent auditors, who determine the reasonableness of the distributions of functional expenses in order to render an unqualified opinion on the financial statements.

Functional Accounting Practices for Public Reporting

The methods described in this appendix will also be useful for other types of financial reporting—e.g., to government agencies, foundations, etc. For example, if a project supported by a government organization or a foundation is conducted within a functional classification that also includes other types of activities, the methods used to accumulate expenses at the "functional level" should also be used to accumulate costs at the "project level" in order to separate the project costs from those of other activities.

Recording Expenses by Function Whenever Possible

Whether expenses are recorded initially on a checkbook stub or in a multicolumn cash disbursements journal, the object expense account of each payment should be indicated at the time it is initially recorded—e.g., supplies, telephone—according to an organization's object expense classification. To facilitate functional accounting for the same expenses, the functional expense account should be entered simultaneously with the object classification whenever possible. It will normally be possible to do so with respect to any expenses incurred for and benefiting only a single function—e.g., supplies for a camp, doctor's fee paid for a client in connection with a single health program. The evident benefits of such point-of-original-entry functional classification of direct expenses are: reduction of month-end analyses, minimization of possible incorrect classifications and establishment of direct documentary evidence supporting an organization's functional classifications.

The attempt to capture all of the management, regulatory and public reporting information at the point-of-original-entry in a large, complex organization can become quite onerous and difficult to administer. The application of ABM and ABC techniques (discussed in more detail below) should be considered where these techniques can result in more accurate information and less complexity of procedures.

Expense Distributable to More Than One Function

The most difficult problem of accounting for expenses by function is posed by expenses that benefit more than one function—e.g., salaries, office rent, travel expenses. Organizations are required to develop techniques that will provide verifiable bases upon which expenses may be related to program or supporting service functions. Many expenses may logically be related to time spent on particular functions—e.g., salaries, travel expenses. Others vary with space used for particular functions: office rent, building depreciation, electricity, heat and janitorial supplies are obvious examples. The identification of equipment used in different functions may provide a logical basis for distributing related depreciation, maintenance, repairs and insurance expenses. If space-related expenses are to be distributed among services using a particular building, it will be necessary to determine the proportion of space used for each function—normally by measurement of floor areas occupied.

Distribution of expenses based on employees' time requires time analysis or time reporting, as will be discussed. Other bases for distribution of expenses may usually be established through a survey, as of space used for different functions, the results of which will furnish a standard basis for distributing related expenses among functions. Organizations experiencing relatively frequent changes in their activities, staff and facilities need to remain alert for changes sufficiently important to require reexamination of established expense-distribution bases. At a minimum, these studies should be updated annually.

Since personal services constitute the largest single cost of most voluntary health and welfare organizations, accounting for staff members' time spent in particular program and supporting services is essential for functional expense reporting by voluntary organizations. For employees whose time is spent exclusively on activities of one program or supporting service, no time reporting

Time Reporting for Functional Expense Accounting

problem exists; their compensation and related expenses such as payroll taxes and employee benefit expenses may be charged directly to the particular service.

Functional expense distribution of compensation of staff members engaged in more than one service during an accounting period requires the accumulation of reliable data upon which such allocations can be made. In some instances, the activities of employees vary considerably throughout the year and from year to year, and thus only the daily time sheet will reasonably reflect the functional distribution. However, accumulation of daily detail time reports for all employees is not required in all instances. Rather, periodic testing of the actual work done by employees in representative job classifications may provide the data needed to determine allocations. The determination and use of a sample distribution does, however, require great care. The periods selected for sampling must be both sufficiently random and of sufficient duration to be statistically representative of an employee's total activities for the year reported upon. In most cases, this will require that sampling procedures be established on a continuing basis. Whenever time reports are kept on a full-time basis or tests made of sampling periods, guidelines should be established reflecting anticipated activities against which the results of the actual time reports may be measured for reasonableness. Employees must be trained in the procedures to be followed in time reporting, and the appropriate functional classification of each of their normal tasks should be discussed with them in advance. In addition, provision should be made for continual monitoring of the time reporting program to detect and correct errors.

In a large and complex nonprofit organization, the diversity of activities may make it impractical to expect employees at every level to understand how their particular activities relate to the highly summarized program and supporting service areas that must be reported to the public. The expense of providing the frequency of training that would be required for both long term and newly hired employees to consistently and accurately apply

Standards of Accounting and Financial Reporting

their time to the appropriate functions could be prohibitive. In such situations application of ABM and ABC techniques can result in higher quality information at less cost and with fewer complexities.

Involvement of Management

The functional classification of expenses permits an organization to tell the reader of the financial statements not only the nature of its expenses, but also the purpose for which they were made. Accordingly, it can never be considered solely a bookkeeping matter. Rather, the organization's management must ensure that the techniques used in accumulating such cost data are adequate and that the results, as reflected in the financial statements, fairly present the actual operations for the year.

The involvement of management in successful ABM/ABC systems is also essential. ABM/ABC can only be fully implemented in organizations that have a clear understanding of the body of activities that are commonly performed (discrete sets of tasks that are managed) in all functional areas. In addition, the organization must have in place sufficient business operating disciplines to allow, for example, a means of identifying the time spent on these activities and a way to relate them to charges in a legacy general ledger system.

A Recommended Procedure for Functional Allocation of Salary Expenses

The following paragraphs illustrate a traditional procedure that has proved workable and is recommended, where size and complexities allow, for adoption by voluntary organizations.

At the time the annual budget is prepared, employees expected to spend their entire time working in one function during the coming year should be identified. Since salaries of these people should be charged directly to the applicable functions, no time sheets are required. However, to assure that their assignments have not changed, a regular, periodic review should be made of their duties and a note entered in the functional allocation documentation that this has been done.

Also at budget time, employees expected to perform work in several functions should be identified. The duties of each employee should then be reviewed and a summary job description prepared, listing both the nature and functional classification of work to be done, and the approximate time to be spent in the respective areas during the coming year. This document should reflect the job tasks in sufficient detail to serve as a reference source for determining proper functional allocations by the employee when preparing time reports. Budgeted allocation percentages should next be prepared for each employee on the basis of this review, together with an understanding of the actual nature of the work to be done as determined by knowledgeable supervisory personnel. In the event that the functional allocation of compensation is to be reflected in the interim financial statements, such allocations may be made on the basis of theses budgeted percentages. The reliability of the budgeted allocation percentages should be verified by the continuing test program of time reporting described below.

Time Reports

Selected employees should be required to submit time reports. In the case of larger organizations, it may be satisfactory to identify representative individuals in each job category, rather than requiring all employees to submit reports.

Frequency of Reports

Time reports of these selected individuals should be required on a regular basis. In most cases, reporting of activities during one week of each month will provide the necessary information to determine whether the work being done is in accordance with that anticipated in the budget, and will at the same time adequately reflect the results of seasonal patterns in work assignments. To assure that the periods are representative, a different week of the month should be selected on a rotating basis.

Staff Training

The individuals designated to submit time reports should be instructed in their preparation. This involves not only a clear understanding of the mechanics of the forms but, more importantly, an adequate understanding of which functions, in an accounting and financial reporting sense, benefit from their individual activities. It is particularly important in this effort that employees recognize that administration of programs and fundraising activities should be charged to those functions and not to management and general.

Report Contents

The time reports should include a brief description of the actual tasks performed, as well as the functions which benefited, and the number of hours spent on each function. Normally, allocation of time to the nearest hour will provide sufficient accuracy for this purpose. All time worked should be accounted for, including overtime and travel time.

Signing and Supervision

Each time report should be reviewed promptly and signed by the supervisor to assure that an examination of the reports has been made for accuracy and representativeness.

Work Sheets Summary

These reports should be summarized on work sheets by an employee. At the year end, the work sheets should be summarized to reflect the total hours and percentages of aggregate time for which reports were submitted, by function, for comparison with the predetermined estimated percentages established at the time the budget was prepared.

Comparison of Actual Percentages

In the event significant variations exist between overall actual percentages and those determined at the time of budget preparations, an investigation should be made and documented to determine the reasons for the variations. If, for example, the assigned duties differ from those that were planned, then it should be determined whether the actual results were representative of the work assigned to all employees in the particular job category. If this is the case, then the predetermined estimates should be revised as appropriate to reflect the actual work done. These revised rates should be used in making the final allocations for the financial statements.

Summary

Obviously, the allocation of salary costs requires the exercise of judgment. The involvement of key management personnel is essential to avoid a strictly mechanical approach, which would result in allocations that do not fairly reflect activities of the organization. It is also essential that there be adequate planning, careful selection and training of employees who submit time reports, and checks on the actual results to ensure that they are reasonable in light of the organization's actual activities.

Samples

Sample time reports and related work sheets are shown on the following pages.

Daily Time Record

Name: _____

Job Title: _____

Date: _____

Description of Work Done	Function Benefited	Number of Hours
_____	Research	_____
_____	Public Education	_____
_____	Professional Education & Training	_____
_____	Patient Services	_____
_____	Community Services	_____
_____	Management & General	_____
_____	Fundraising	_____
_____	TOTAL WORKED HOURS	_____

_____
Supervisor Approval

Annual Time Allocation Summary

Name: _____

Job Title: _____

Week Beginning	Total Hours	Research	Public Education	Professional Education & Training	Patient Services	Community Services	Management & General	Fund-Raising
Annual Hours								
Actual %								
Estimated %								
Difference								

The activities based management and costing model is intended to mitigate the complexities involved in meeting the diverse financial reporting requirements typically encountered by most non-profit organizations. A successful ABM/ABC model must be customized to meet the management needs of each non-profit organization. Accordingly, the purpose of the following section is to describe the conceptual framework of an ABM/ABC model in terms of its objectives, advantages, and disadvantages. non-profit organizations (especially those with numerous and diverse activities) are encouraged to evaluate ABM/ABC as a viable alternative to attempting to accommodate diverse and frequent changing financial reporting requirements through the traditional means of a complex, multi-level chart of accounts structure.

Key Advantages of the ABM/ABC Model

- Implementation of ABM/ABC forces management to articulate a clear understanding of the body of activities (discrete set of managed tasks) that are commonly performed in all functional areas. Consequently, ABM/ABC enhances management's ability to evaluate the effectiveness of these activities in terms of end results and at what cost.

- Reduces administrative complexities by limiting the accounting system structure to two dimensions . . . (a) the traditional line item account codes for assets, liabilities, net assets, revenues, and natural expenses categories, and (b) activity codes that classify revenues and expenses for reporting by functions, grants, projects, cost centers, responsibility centers, or any other cost objective that represents a discrete set of managed tasks over which the organization desires accountability.

- ABM/ABC facilitates the development of reasonable cost allocation methods and at the same time avoids establishing costly and burdensome allocation procedures.

Activities Based Management (ABM) and Activities Based Costing (ABC) Model

- Cost allocation procedures are developed at a responsible management level by staff who are trained and understand the relationship among the organization's products, programs, and supporting services; and can be held accountable for the activities.

- ABM/ABC are consistent with the cost allocation guidance found in OMB circular A-122, IRS 990, and authoritative GAAP accounting literature.

Possible Obstacles to the ABM/ABC Model

ABM/ABC may not lend itself as well to staff time-keeping on a sampling basis especially for organizations that work cross-functionally. While ABM/ABC simplifies most aspects of cost allocations and diverse financial reporting requirements; a key element of a successful system is the ability to maintain detailed, verifiable staff time records. Depending upon the complexity of the non-profit organization's activities, it may be necessary for the non-profit organization to adopt disciplined business practices for staff time accountability.

On the positive side, maintenance of detailed, verifiable staff time records is a specific requirement of OMB Circular A-122. Accordingly, any non-profit organization accepting government funding should already meet this requirement.

Illustration of an Investment Pool

APPENDIX

2

Three Funds (A, B, and C) combined their cash some years ago into an investment pool by simultaneous contributions (in the portions indicated below) totaling $90,000, which was invested. On December 31, 19X5, the pooled investments on a cost basis were carried at $100,000, the original contributions plus $10,000 representing net realized gains retained by the investment pool.

The market value of the pooled assets was calculated to be $150,000. On this basis, the unrealized net gains are $50,000.

A new Fund (Fund D) puts $100,000 in cash into the investment pool at December 31, 19X5.

The following table presents the transactions set forth above and illustrates the calculation of the resulting equity percentages:

Fund	Cash Originally Contributed to Pool	Original Equity Percentage	Value of Pool on December 31, 19XX		Value After Entry of Fund D	New Equity Percentage
			Cost	Market		
A	$40,000	44.44%	$ 44,444	$ 66,667	$ 66,667	26.67%
B	35,000	38.89	38,889	58,333	58,333	23.33
C	15,000	16.67	16,667	25,000	25,000	10.00
D	—	—	—	—	100,000	40.00
	$90,000	100.00%	$100,000	$150,000	$250,000	100.00%

If Fund A were to withdraw from the investment pool at this date, it would be entitled to $66,667 rather than $44,444. The equity percentages to be used for entries to and withdrawals from the pool are based on market values, even though the accounting records may be kept on a cost basis.

Internal Control over Contributions

All organizations have a responsibility to ensure that appropriate internal accounting controls are established and maintained over all categories of contributions. Simply defined, internal control is a system of procedures and cross-checking which, in the absence of collusion, both minimizes the likelihood of misappropriation of assets or misstatement of the accounts, and maximizes the likelihood of prompt detection and assignment of responsibility if they do occur.

The objectives of internal accounting control for nonprofit organizations generally are the same as the objectives for profit-oriented organizations. Some characteristics of nonprofit organizations that influence internal accounting control include:

- A volunteer governing board, many of whose members serve for limited terms.

- A limited number of staff personnel, sometimes too few to provide the appropriate segregation of duties.

- A mixture of volunteers and employees participating in operations. Depending on the size and other features of the organization, day-to-day operations sometimes are conducted by volunteers instead of employees. The manner in which responsibility and authority are delegated varies among organizations. This may affect control over financial transactions, particularly with respect to authorization.

- A budget approved by the governing board. The budget may serve as authorization for the activities to be carried out by management in attaining the organization's program objectives. Nonprofit organizations should prepare budgets for both operating and capital expenditures.

Establishing internal control over contributions is often difficult, particularly where a gap exists between the time and place a contribution is originally made—e.g., to a door-to-door solicitor—and the time it is recorded in the books in the organization's office. Nevertheless, each organization must carefully consider its responsibility to establish appropriate internal controls. The AICPA Voluntary Health and Welfare audit guide requires the independent public accountant who believes internal controls are not adequate to issue a qualified opinion.

The audit guide discusses those internal control procedures normally appropriate over various types of contributions, including mail campaigns, door-to-door solicitation, etc. The audit guide notes, for instance, that "two employees should be assigned the function of jointly controlling incoming mail and preparing a record of amounts received. This record should be routinely compared with the bank deposits, preferably by someone not having access to the donations." Similar controls are indicated for other types of solicitation.

Each organization should discuss with its independent public accountant its system of internal accounting control over contributions to ensure that the organization is fulfilling its responsibilities. This will not only help to protect the organization but will also avoid placing the independent public accountant in the position of having to qualify the opinion due to inadequate internal controls. Also at stake is public confidence, if it is disclosed that an organization does not employ reasonable and prudent safeguards in controlling contributed funds.

Summarized below are procedures that will assist organizations in establishing practical, cost-effective controls. The control procedures listed below are not intended to be all-inclusive or necessarily applicable to every situation. However, where basic sources of receipts exist, the procedures outlined can be adapted to just about any situation, depending on the number of employees and type of existing control and accounting systems. Therefore, to the extent possible, the control procedures below should be implemented.

Effective control over mail receipts is essential. Control may be achieved by procedures such as the following:

Mail Receipts

- Joint control of mail received by the organization—two or more persons (1) jointly control and open all incoming mail, (2) restrictively endorse checks immediately—including the number of the bank account in which the funds will be deposited, (3) prepare a list, in duplicate, of amounts received, (4) sign the list to attest to its accuracy, and (5) send one copy of the list to the organization's accounting department for recording in the accounting records, and send the second copy of the list, with the cash receipts, to the person responsible for making the bank deposit (who should be independent of the accounting function). A person who does not have access to cash receipts compares the bank deposit record with the accounting department cash receipts record.

- Use of a bank or other lock box service—the organization's fund-raising solicitations direct that contributions by mail be sent to a post office box. The recipient opens the mail, deposits the receipts, and furnishes the organization with a list of the lock box receipts and an authenticated deposit slip. If a lock box service is used, the organization should periodically ascertain that internal controls at the service are adequate and in effect. This may include requesting a letter to that effect from the independent auditor of the service. Also, prior to selection of a bank or "caging" operation to provide lock box services, an organization should ask for a current customer list so references can be checked, and should also request a tour of the operation to ensure that adequate controls exist.

The following procedures are sometimes used to supplement internal accounting controls over contributions received by mail:

- An outside organization may make test mailings of "contributions" that are subsequently traced into the records.

- An outside fund-raising service, having no access to cash receipts, may handle the mailing of all fund-raising literature and follow up on lack of adequate responses to campaigns.

- An organization may initiate confirmation procedures using previous contributor listings as the selection population.

Direct Contact Solicitations

If direct contact campaigns are conducted, the following are important controls:

- Appropriate supervision of the solicitors. This often is accomplished by a pyramid structure of area chairmen, division captains, neighborhood captains and door-to-door solicitors, with each level reporting to the next higher level.

- Restriction of solicitation materials to authorized solicitors. This may involve a specific form of identification authorizing them to solicit contributions for the organization.

- Separation of physical control of cash from the accounting control over the contributions received. This separation should be achieved at the earliest possible point. For example, a door-to-door solicitor should submit a report to the neighborhood captain. The report should reconcile the contributions received (some of which may be in the form of pledges) with the cash collected. The solicitor should also send a copy of the report directly to the organization's accounting department to establish accounting control and to permit later comparison with the amounts deposited.

- Minimization of the number of persons having access to cash and of the amount of cash in any one person's control. The cash collected should be deposited in a bank at the earliest practical time by a designated person (such as by the neighborhood captain).

- The use of fund-raising reports to check the results of each solicitation against street maps or other controls, to ascertain that all areas and all solicitors have been accounted for.

- The use of prenumbered receipts, sponsor sheets, summary reports, etc., to ensure that all documents and related receipts are properly accounted for.

- Preparation of summaries of all fund-raising reports, reconciliation of all reports with the organization's records and comparison of the recorded amounts with total bank deposits.

- Accounting for all sealed containers that are used to collect cash.

Other internal accounting control procedures that may be appropriate for cash contributions include the following:

Other Control Procedures

- Use of procedures similar to those for incoming mail to control the counting of the contents of sealed containers or of open plate collections. Containers, once collected, and open plate collections should be maintained under the joint control of two or more responsible persons until they are counted. The practice of using unattended, moveable collection receptacles such as canisters or boxes is discouraged because incoming receipts are difficult to control and are subject to misdirection, misuse or theft.

- Establishment of separate accountabilities for donor-restricted gifts to appropriately classify and account for them and to monitor compliance with donor restrictions.

- Use of prenumbered contribution acknowledgment forms, when practicable.

- Maintenance of a record of gifts contingent on future events (such as bequests), which is reviewed periodically.

- Budgeting of contributions that can reasonably be estimated, and investigation of differences between actual contributions and such budgeted amounts or prior year amounts.

- Restrictive endorsement (for example: "for deposit only to the account of XYZ organization, account #65893 of First State Bank") of all checks received by the organization immediately upon receipt to prevent the deposit of such checks in unauthorized bank accounts.

- Publication of donors' names in a journal or program, and investigation of complaints from donors whose names were omitted or the amount of whose gifts did not agree. The investigator should be a person who is independent of the contribution receiving and recording functions.

Standards of Accounting and Financial Reporting

Reporting of Service Efforts and Accomplishments

As previously noted, Concepts Statement No. 4 suggests that service efforts and accomplishments information is useful in assessing an organization's performance. Such information is useful because accomplishments of not-for-profit organizations generally cannot be measured solely by traditional financial indicators, and because resource providers who are not beneficiaries or recipients of an organization's services often do not have direct knowledge about an organization's outputs.

Service efforts generally refer to inputs—money, personnel and materials—which comprise the costs of providing programs and services. Most organizations present service efforts information in their financial statements through functional expense reporting. Service accomplishments generally refer to outputs—goods or services produced and program results. Techniques for reporting this information are generally less developed than those for service efforts, and, for that reason, FASB Concepts Statement No. 4 uses the qualifying language *"ideally* [emphasis added] financial reporting also should provide information about the service accomplishments of a nonbusiness organization."

In 1980, the FASB published the results of a study commissioned by the board to review not-for-profit organizations' financial reports and to record and classify instances in which the organizations reported their performance using service efforts and accomplishments information. The study concluded that most service efforts and accomplishments reporting was done in reports other than general purpose external financial reports. In addition, information about efforts was more prevalent than information about accomplishments. Information about results was noted less frequently, and the study suggested that additional research in the area should be encouraged. Currently, the Governmental Accounting Standards Board is studying the topic.

Until additional research on the topic is completed, no standards on reporting service accomplishments will be issued. Nevertheless, organizations are encouraged to experiment with presenting this information with the objective of improving the communication of their achievements to constituencies.

Accounting for Costs of Activities That Include Fund-Raising

As discussed in Chapter 4 and in accordance with AICPA SOP 98-2 released in March, 1998, in certain circumstances, voluntary health and welfare organizations should allocate the joint costs of informational materials and activities that include a fund-raising appeal between the fund-raising function and the appropriate program or management and general function.

This appendix has been prepared to provide some insights into these issues. While many questions undoubtedly will continue to plague those who must deal with this matter, it is hoped that the examples offered below will contribute to the achievement of the goal that well-intentioned individuals arrive at reasonably the same conclusions when faced with the same facts. This will help to retain and enhance the credibility of the financial reports presented to the contributing public by voluntary health and welfare organizations.

SOP 98-2[1]

Illustrations of Applying the Criteria of Purpose, Audience and Content to Determine Whether a Program or Management and General Activity Has Been Conducted.

Illustration 1

Facts

Entity A's mission is to prevent drug abuse. Entity A's annual report states that one of its objectives in fulfilling that mission is to assist parents in preventing their children from abusing drugs.

---

1. Reprinted with permission from AICPA, Copyright © 1998 by the American Institute of Certified Public Accounts, Inc.

Entity A mails informational materials to the parents of all junior high school students explaining the prevalence and dangers of drug abuse. The materials encourage parents to counsel children about the dangers of drug abuse and inform them about how to detect drug abuse. The mailing includes a request for contributions. Entity A conducts other activities informing the public about the dangers of drug abuse and encouraging parents to counsel their children about drug abuse that do not include requests for contributions and that are conducted in different media. Entity A's executive director is involved in the development of the informational materials as well as the request for contributions. The executive director's annual compensation includes a significant bonus if total annual contributions exceed a predetermined amount.

Conclusion

The purpose, audience, and content criteria are met, and the joint costs should be allocated.

The activity calls for specific action by the recipient (encouraging parents to counsel children about the dangers of drug abuse and informing them about how to detect drug abuse) that will help accomplish the entity's mission. Neither of the compensation nor similar activity factors is determinative of whether the purpose criterion is met. (Although entity A's executive director's annual compensation varies based on annual contributions, the executive director's compensation does not vary based on contributions raised for this discrete joint activity.) The purpose criterion is met based on the other evidence, because (a) the program component of this activity calls for specific action by the recipient (encouraging parents to counsel children about the dangers of drugs abuse) that will help accomplish the entity's mission, and it otherwise conducts the program activity in this illustration without a request for contributions, and (b) performing such programs helps accomplish Entity A's mission. (Note that had Entity A conducted the activity using the same medium on a scale that is similar to or greater than the scale on which it is conducted with the request for contributions, the purpose criterion would have been met and it would not have been necessary to consider other evidence.)

The audience criterion is met because the audience (parents of junior high school students) is selected based on its need to use or reasonable potential for use of the action called for by the program component.

The content criterion is met because the activity calls for specific action by the recipient (encouraging parents to counsel children about the dangers of drug abuse and informing them about how to detect drug abuse) that will help accomplish the entity's mission (assisting parents in preventing their children from abusing drugs), and it explains the need for the benefits of the action (the prevalence and dangers of drug abuse).

Illustration 2

Facts

Entity's B's mission is to reduce the incidence of illness for ABC disease, which afflicts a broad segment of the population. One of Entity B's objectives in fulfilling that mission is to inform the public about the effects and early warning signs of the disease and specific action that should be taken to prevent the disease.

Entity B maintains a list of its prior donors and sends them donor renewal mailings. The mailings include messages about the effects and early warning signs of the disease and specific action that should be taken to prevent it. That information is also sent to a similar-sized audience but without the request for contributions. Also, Entity B believes that recent donors are more likely to contribute than non-donors or donors who have not contributed recently. Prior donors are deleted from the mailing list if they have not contributed to Entity B recently, and new donors are added to the list. There is no evidence of a correlation between recent contributions and participation in the program component of the activity. Also, the prior donors' need to use or reasonable potential for use of the messages about the effects and early warning signs of the disease and specific action that should be taken to prevent it is an insignificant factor in their selection.

Conclusion

The purpose and content criteria are met. The audience criterion is not met. All costs, including those that might otherwise be considered program or management and general costs if they had been incurred in a different activity, should be charged to fund raising.

The activity calls for specific action by the recipient (action that should be taken to prevent ABC disease) that will help accomplish the entity's mission. The purpose criterion is met because (a) the program component of the activity calls for specific action by the recipient that will help accomplish the entity's mission (to reduce the incidence of illness from the disease), and (b) the program is also conducted using the same medium on a scale that is similar to or greater than the scale on which it is conducted with the request for contributions (a similar mailing is done without the request for contributions, to a similar sized audience).

The audience criterion is not met. The rebuttable presumption that the audience criterion is not met because the audience includes prior donors is not overcome in this illustration. Although the audience has a need to use or reasonable potential for use of the program component, that was an insignificant factor in its selection.

The content criterion is met because the activity calls for specific action by the recipient (actions to prevent ABC disease) that will help accomplish the entity's mission (to reduce the incidence of ABC disease), and it explains the need for and benefits of the action (to prevent ABC disease).

Illustration 3

Facts

Entity C's mission is to reduce the incidence of illness from ABC disease, which afflicts a broad segment of the population. One of Entity C's objectives in fulfilling that mission is to increase governmental funding for research about ABC disease.

Entity C maintains a list of its prior donors and its employees call them on the telephone reminding them of the effects of ABC disease, asking for contributions, and encouraging them to contact their elected officials to urge increase governmental funding for research about ABC disease. The callers are educated about ABC, do not otherwise perform fund-raising functions, and are not compensated or evaluated based on contributions raised. Entity C's research indicates that recent donors are likely to contact their elected officials about such funding while nonrecent donors are not. Prior donors are deleted from the calling list if they have not contributed to Entity C recently, and new donors are added to the list.

Conclusion

The purpose, audience, and content criteria are met, and the joint costs should be allocated.

The activity calls for specific action by the recipient (contacting elected officials concerning funding for research about ABC disease) that will help accomplish the entity's mission. Neither of the compensation nor the similar activity factors is determinative of whether the purpose criterion is met. Therefore, other evidence should be considered. The purpose criterion is met based on the other evidence, because (a) the qualifications and duties of the personnel performing the activity indicate that it is a program activity (the callers are educated about ABC and do not otherwise perform fund-raising functions), (b) the method of compensation for performing the activity (the employees are not compensated or evaluated based on contributions raised), and (c) performing such programs helps accomplish Entity C's mission.

The audience criterion is met because the audience (recent donors) is selected based on its ability to assist Entity C in meeting the goals of the program component of the activity (recent donors are likely to contact their elected officials about such funding while nonrecent donors are not).

The content criterion is met because the activity calls for specific action by recipient (contacting elected officials concerning funding for research about ABC disease) that will help accomplish the entity's mission (to reduce the incidence or ABC disease), and it explains the need for and benefits of the action (to prevent ABC disease).

Illustration 4

Facts

Entity D's mission is to improve the quality of life for senior citizens. One of Entity D's objectives included in that mission is to increase the physical activity of senior citizens. One of Entity D's programs to attain that objective is to send representatives to speak to groups about the importance of exercise and to conduct exercise classes.

Entity D mails a brochure on the importance of exercise that encourages exercise in later years to residents over the age of sixty-five in three zip code areas. The last two pages of the four-page brochure include a perforated contribution remittance form on which Entity D explains its program and makes an appeal for contributions. The content of the first two pages of the brochure is primarily educational; it explains how seniors can undertake a self-supervised exercise program and encourages them to undertake such a program. In addition, Entity D includes a second brochure on various exercise techniques that can be used by those undertaking an exercise program.

The brochures are distributed to educate people in this age group about the importance of exercising, to help them exercise properly, and to raise contributions for Entity D. These objectives are documented in a letter to the public relations firm that developed the brochures. The audience is selected based on age, without regard to ability to contribute. Entity D believes that most of the recipients would benefit from the information about exercise.

Conclusion

The purpose, audience, and content criteria are met, and the joint costs should be allocated. (Note that the costs of the second brochure should be charged to program because all the costs of the brochure are identifiable with the program function.)

The activity calls for specific action by the recipient (exercising) that will help accomplish the entity's mission. Neither the compensation nor the similar activity is determinative of whether the purpose criterion is met. Therefore, other evidence should be considered. The purpose criterion is met based on the other evidence, because (a) performing such programs helps accomplish Entity D's mission, and (b) the objectives of the program are documented in a letter to the public relations firm that developed the brochure.

The audience criterion is met because the audience (residents over sixty-five is certain zip codes) is selected based on its need to use or reasonable potential for use of the action called for by the program component.

The content criterion is met because the activity calls for specific action by the recipient (exercising) that will help accomplish the entity's mission (increasing the physical activity of senior citizens), and the need for and benefits of the action are clearly evident (explains the importance of exercising).

Illustration 5

Facts

The facts are the same as those in Illustration 4, except that Entity E employs a fund-raising consultant to develop the first brochure and pays that consultant 30 percent of contributions raised.

Conclusion

The content and audience criteria are met. The purpose criterion is not met, however, because a majority of compensation or fees for the fund-raising consultant varies based on contributions raised for this discrete joint activity (the fund-raising consultant is paid 30 percent of contributions raised). All costs should be charged to fund raising, including the costs of the second brochure and any other costs that otherwise might be considered program or management and general costs if they had been incurred in a different activity.

Illustration 6

Facts

Entity G's mission is to provide summer camps for economically disadvantaged youths. Educating the families of ineligible youths about the camps is not one of the program objectives included in that mission.

Entity G conducts a door-to-door solicitation campaign for its camp programs. In the campaign, volunteers with canisters visit homes in middle-class neighborhoods to collect contributions. Entity G believes that people in those neighborhoods would not need the camp's program but may contribute. The volunteers explain the camp's programs, including why the disadvantages children benefit from the program, and distribute leaflets to the residents regardless of whether they contribute to the camp. The leaflets describe the camp, its activities, who can attend, and the benefits to attendees. Requests for contributions are not included in the leaflets.

Conclusion

The activity does not include a call for specific action because it only educates the audience about causes (describing the camp, its activities, who can attend, and the benefits to attendees). Therefore, the purpose criterion is not met.

The audience criterion is not met, because the audience is selected based on its ability or likelihood to contribute, rather than based on (a) its need to use or reasonable potential for use of the action called for by the program component, or (b) its ability to take action to assist the entity in meeting the goals of the program component of the activity. (Entity G believes that people in those neighborhoods would not need the camp's programs but may contribute.)

The content criterion is not met because the activity does not call for specific action by the recipient. (The content educates the audience about causes that the program is designed to address without calling for specific action.)

Illustration 7

Facts

Entity H's mission is to educate the public about lifesaving techniques in order to increase the number of lives saved. One of Entity H's objectives in fulfilling that mission, as stated in the minutes of the board's meetings, is to produce and show television broadcasts including information about lifesaving techniques.

Entity H conducts an annual national telethon to raise contributions and to reach the American public with lifesaving educational messages, such as summary instructions concerning dealing with certain life-threatening situations. Based on the information communicated by the messages, the need for and benefits of the action are clearly evident. The broadcast includes segments describing Entity H's services. Entity H broadcasts the telethon to the entire country, not merely to areas selected on the basis of giving potential or prior fund raising results. Also, Entity H uses national television broadcasts devoted entirely to lifesaving educational messages to conduct program activities without fund-raising.

Conclusion

The purpose, audience, and content criteria are met, and the joint costs should be allocated.

The activity calls for specific action by the recipient (implicitly—to save lives) that will help accomplish the entity's mission. The purpose criterion is met because (a) the program component of the activity calls for specific action by the recipient that will help accomplish Entity H's mission (to save lives by educating the public), and (b) a similar program activity is conducted without the fund-raising using the same medium and on a scale that is similar to or greater than the scale on which it is conducted with the appeal (Entity H uses national television broadcasts devoted entirely to lifesaving educational messages to conduct program activities without fund raising).

The audience criterion is met because the audience (a broad segment of the population) is selected based on its need to use or reasonable potential for use of the action called for by the program activity.

The content criterion is met because the activity calls for specific action by the recipient (implicitly—to save lives) that will help accomplish the entity's mission (to saves lives by educating the public), and the need for and benefits of the action are clearly evident (saving lives is desirable).

Illustration 8

Facts

Entity I's mission is to provide food, clothing, and medical care to children in developing countries.

Entity I conducts television broadcasts in the United States that describe its programs, show the needy children, and end with appeals for contributions. Entity I's operating policies and internal management memoranda state that these programs are designed to educate the public about the needs of children in developing countries and to raise contributions. The employees producing the programs are trained in audiovisual production and are familiar with Entity I's program. Also, the executive producer is paid $25,000 for the activity, with $5,000 bonus if the activity raises over $1,000,000.

Conclusion

The purpose, audience, and content criteria are not met. All costs should be charged to fund-raising.

The activity does not include a call for specific action because it only educates the audience about causes (describing its programs and showing the needy children). Therefore, the purpose criterion is not met. (Also, note that if the compensation factor were considered, it would not be determinative of whether the purpose criterion is met. Although the executive producer will be paid $5,000 if the activity raises over $1,000,000, that amount would not be a majority of the executive producer's total compensation for this activity, because $5,000 would not be a majority of the executive producer's total compensation of $30,000 for this activity. Also, note that if other evidence were considered, the purpose criterion would not be met based on other evidence. Although the qualifications and duties of the personnel performing the activity indicate that the employees producing the program are familiar with Entity I's programs, the facts that some, but less than a majority, of the executive producer's compensation varies based on contributions raised, and that the operating policies and internal management memoranda state that these programs are designed to educate the public about the needs of children in developing countries (with no call for specific action by recipients) and to raise contributions, indicate that the purpose is fund raising.)

The audience criterion is not met because the audience is selected based on its ability or likelihood to contribute, rather than based on (a) its need to use or reasonable potential for use of the action called for by the program component, or (b) its ability to take action to assist the entity in meeting the goal of the program component of the activity. (The audience is a broad segment of the population of a country that is not in need of or has no reasonable potential for use of the program activity.)

The content criterion is not met because the activity does not call for specific action by the recipient that will help accomplish the entity's mission. (The content educates the audience about the causes without calling for specific action.)

Illustration 9

Facts

Entity J is a university that distributes its annual report, which includes reports on mission accomplishments, to those who have made significant contributions over previous year, its board of trustees, and its employees. The annual report is primarily prepared by management and general personnel, such as the accounting department and executive staff. The activity is coordinated by the public relations department. Internal management memoranda indicate that the purpose of the annual report is to report on how management discharged its stewardship responsibilities, including the university's overall performance, goals, financial position, cash flows, and results of operations. Included in the package containing the annual report are requests for contributions and donor reply cards.

Conclusion

The purpose, audience, and content criteria are met, and the joint costs should be allocated.

The activity has elements of management and general functions. Therefore, no call for specific action is required. Neither of the compensation or similar activity factors is determinative of whether the purpose criterion is met. Therefore, other evidence should be considered. The purpose criterion is met based on the other evidence, because (a) the employees performing the activity are not members of the fund-raising activities and (b) internal management memoranda indicate that the purpose of the annual report is to fulfill one of the university's management and general responsibilities.

The audience criterion is met because the audience is selected based on its reasonable potential for use of the management and general component. Although the activity is directed primarily at those who have previously made significant contributions, the audience was selected based on its presumed interest in Entity J's annual report (prior donors who have made significant contributions are likely to have an interest in matters discussed in the annual report.)

The content criterion is met because the activity (distributing annual reports) fulfills one of the entity's management and general responsibilities (reporting concerning management's fulfillment of its stewardship function.)

Illustration 10

Facts

Entity L is an animal rights organization. It mails a package of material to individuals included in lists rented from various environmental and other organizations that support causes that Entity L believes are congruent with its own. In addition to donor response cards and return envelopes, the package includes (a) materials urging recipients to contact their legislators and urge the legislators to support legislation to protect those rights, and (b) postcards addressed to legislators urging support for legislation restricting the use of animal testing for cosmetic products. The mail campaign is part of an overall strategy that includes magazine advertisements and the distribution of similar materials at various community events, some of which are undertaken without fund-raising appeals. The advertising and community events reach audiences similar in size and demographics to the audience reached by the mailing.

Conclusion

The purpose, audience, and content criteria are met, and the joint costs should be allocated.

The activity calls for specific action by the recipient (mailing postcards to legislators urging support for legislation restricting the use of animal testing for cosmetic products) that will help accomplish the entity's mission. Neither of the compensation or the similar activity factors is determinative of whether the purpose criterion is met. Therefore, other evidence, should be considered. The purpose criterion is met based on the other evidence, because (a) the program component of this activity calls for specific action by the recipient that will help accomplish the entity's mission, and it otherwise conducts the program activity in this illustration without a request for contributions, and (b) performing such programs helps accomplish Entity L's mission.

The audience criterion is met because the audience (individuals included in lists rented from various environmental and other organizations that support causes that Entity L believes are congruent with it own) is selected based on its ability to take action to assist the entity in meeting the goals of the program component of the activity.

The content criterion is met because the activity calls for specific action by the recipient (mailing postcards to legislator urging support for legislation restricting the use of animal testing for cosmetic products) that will help accomplish the entity's mission (to protect animal rights), and the need for and benefits of the action are clearly evident (to protect animal rights).

Index

Standards of Accounting and Financial Reporting